It's the system that's broken, not your child

SARAH TAYLOR

For our beautiful daughters
Maisie and Poppy

For my amazing husband Arron who gave me the
self-belief to write this book

And for my precious parents who have believed in me
and given me the wisdom that lives through these pages

Acknowledgements

I am forever grateful to so many people who I have worked with over the many years to trust me with their life stories. You have shared personal experiences of education, both the positives and negatives that have inspired me to write this book and bring back the faith that education can be and should be a positive experience.

Thank you to my big sister Rachel for all your support and invaluable feedback.

Thanks to Cameron for your enthusiasm, praise and drive which encouraged me to complete this project.

Finally, thank you to Karen for your amazing copyediting and proofreading, along with your boosts of energy and confidence for the content to be published.

"Everybody is a genius,
but if you judge a fish by its ability to climb a tree,
it will live its whole life believing it is stupid."

Albert Einstein

Contents

Preface

As a little girl, one of my favourite games was playing teacher, spending hours calling register, checking homework, whilst ensuring my class paid attention to me writing on my chalkboard with the occasional teddy bear being reprimanded for bad behaviour. However, the reality of my real personal experiences of education as an adolescent and teen were very different, and in fact most of the time I struggled through the schooling system feeling disengaged to a great extent. I would go as far as to say I was disconnected from the education process and merely turned up, did what I had to do and then went home to a life that was much more pleasant for me.

Many years later, at the age of 25, I had a life-affirming 'lightbulb moment'. My employer elected me to attend a

Leadership Training Programme to learn how to manage my team effectively, and for the first time in my life I discovered that I not only assimilated the content of the course easily, I actually really enjoyed the learning. As mentioned, this was by stark contrast to my journey through the education system.

By the age of 27, I finally discovered what I loved doing; training and developing people to be the very best that they possibly could be, something I had and still have a real passion for. Driven by the fact that I personally found how rewarding it was when you realise you can actually be great at something. This, without a doubt, is what I love about my professional career; helping people to feel fantastic about themselves and tapping into their raw talent. How have I done this? Through identifying the natural attributes of the many thousands of people I have had the pleasure of working with, enabling them with the skills, knowledge, and behaviours to excel in their professional careers. Designing exciting learning initiatives that not only have targeted outcomes but are most definitely enjoyable and makes the content or subject matter stimulating to learn about.

All of us remember school; the fantastic engaging teachers who used experiential learning methods and fun activities to accelerate the learning process, and the dull repetitive lessons where we could not wait for the class to finish. If you want students to take away key learning points that they will apply to their live environments, the teaching methods have to be interesting and enjoyable with a common thread as to how this is applied in their worlds. Creating material that is dull and monotonous learning will result in bored, disengaged pupils, and could possibly lead to other challenges such as disruptive and agitated behaviour.

The truth is children, like adults and vice versa, all learn in different ways; content and delivery styles that engage one learner may have a disconnect with the next. Why? Simply because we are all unique. Based on this, it is critical we consider all ways of learning to maintain interest, involvement, and retention.

Between 1998 and 1999, I attained my Certificates in both Training Practice and Training Design from the Chartered Institute of Personnel and Development and have been an Associate Member of the CIPD ever since. These qualifications have undoubtedly helped me bring validity, credibility and contributed to the success of many organisations I have supported to develop their people.

Being a mother of two daughters, and having first-hand experiences of both the education system and what employers really want from their people, it never ceases to amaze me how antiquated our schooling system really is – not to mention the resultant effects it can have on our children. This is what compelled me to write *Unbrand My Child*.

In this book, I explore many avenues of how the system works currently and how it could easily be improved. Most importantly, I hope *Unbrand My Child* enables parents to see all the attributes their children really do have if time is taken to tap into their raw talents.

Unfortunately, we still have a system that was designed to meet the needs of the Industrial Revolution. With unattainable measures for most teachers to ever dream of achieving with the mix of pupils they teach, leading inevitably and sadly to disillusion in far too many cases.

Our children are scrutinised through a microscope to see what they cannot do, rather than what they can, causing long-lasting effects and, in some cases, mental health issues that they will carry with them for the rest of their lives. I regularly experience this as I teach and coach these people as grown-ups and know that if their earlier education had been successful in building their self-belief and esteem, these individuals could have achieved far greater things for themselves in their earlier careers. Creating a sense of belonging for people to undertake education, rather than a feeling from them that they are not worthy.

After reading this book I hope you take comfort from understanding that your child is amazing – but then you know that anyway!

We just need to mend the broken system.

Chapter One

Negative Branding

*"If you're not prepared to be wrong,
You'll never come up with anything original."*

Sir Ken Robinson

Imagine if the world believed that being intelligent and bright stretched far beyond education, exams, and results. That we believed that all children are clever, and all children can achieve success by using their raw talent.

We all know and recognise talent and unique attributes, however acknowledgement of them in relation to somebody being 'bright' is too often overlooked.

If we think that **'behind every child who believes in themselves, was somebody, whether it was a parent, guardian, teacher or friend, who believed in them first...'** it follows that if we widen our view on what we believe to be intelligent, then we may just grow our children into happier adults. With a childhood full of wonderful things that met their raw capabilities and talents, they were made to feel great about who they really are at the most fundamental level, individualism.

Let us explore the concept of somebody being able to make somebody else happy, purely through the way they interact. We all know people who have a talent for making people feel happy. They may have such a great sense of humour that they naturally make others feel wonderful when they are around them. Maybe you are already thinking of people who do this, we certainly know that not everybody can.

If we take the fact that all children have talents, this book explores how we could recognise those talents to make them as important as achievement and attainment, thus ensuring that we find their inner happiness and wellbeing, grow it, and the child excels.

Living in a world of inclusion, it never ceases to amaze me how we still have an education system built on exclusion. In fact, if we ran our businesses in this way, not only would we find ourselves in court constantly, we would probably have many more failed organisations and businesses, as success is achieved by having diverse ideas and talents in all walks of life.

Everybody needs to know their self-worth to be completely happy, so why do we not spend our time exploring what children can do, rather than what they cannot.

Concentrating on what a child can do, will always create a deeper level of contentment and almost certainly a more confident, well-adjusted adult.

With self-worth being the primary driver behind unleashing raw potential and growing the world around the child rather than our child around the world.

What does that really mean? Ensuring we adapt to get the best out of our child's raw talent. After all, if you asked a monkey to swim up-stream, it would fail; however, to swing from a tree it would, without a doubt, succeed.

Although it is healthy for everybody to know and understand their limitations, surely by concentrating the majority of efforts on areas for personal development, rather than areas of strength, we run the risk of creating many limiting beliefs and feelings. In turn, these beliefs and feelings can become stifling as children develop into adult life.

As parents who love our children, we want to feel proud, and more importantly we all want the best for them. We want our children to be happy in all aspects of their life, which is one of the reasons we want them to achieve well at school, enabling them to get a 'good' education.

What do you hope for? 'Happy', 'successful' or 'talented', never 'anxious', 'sad' or 'depressed'.

In the initial stages of development, babies constantly yearn for physical and social interaction, whether that is touching your hand, a comforter or blankie, focussing on everything. Like all animals they learn from the moment they are born. Their innate behaviours are programmed to learn and enjoy interaction at all levels, from physical practical role-play through to auditory and visual observations. This does not change with age.

In general terms, parents have children to provide love and most definitely positive attention.

Out of school hours we watch and encourage recreational activities such as cycling, running, swimming, climbing trees, joining groups and teams, all to grow our beautiful children into well-balanced, content adults.

An interesting observation of mine was when I went to my daughter's school to watch her singing in the choir, something that many schools consider important.

For so many, singing, music and dance brings out emotion and contentment. In fact, a study by researchers from McGill University in Montreal explored how the chemical dopamine had been tested in response to music. The study, reported in a scientific monthly journal *Nature Neuroscience*, confirmed that the chemical was released at moments of peak enjoyment.

The report authors say it's significant in proving that humans obtain an abstract reward and pleasure from music, that is comparable with the pleasure obtained from more basic biological stimuli.

In this study, levels of dopamine were found to be up to 9% higher when volunteers were listening to music they enjoyed.

Often people relate music to events that have happened in their lifetime, creating high levels of emotion. There can be nothing wrong with creating the 'feel-good factor' in life, creating positive energy for so many.

Of course, the main issue with this is the question of how much time should be spent on singing, when at the end of the day, academic subjects will get them a better job! Or potentially anyway.

If you think when your child was a toddler, songs and rhymes were probably very much part of their early development and as we know can be a release of so many tensions, so surely to continue this into juniors, seniors and adult life can only be a positive for many growing adolescents.

During my daughter's concert, it was wonderful to see the youngsters on the stage booming out their lovely notes and suddenly delighted to see the younger children in the audience starting to jig and rock to the rhythm. To my amazement the teacher was signalling them to sit still. Sit completely still to the singing and music. I supposed this is a kind of 'crowd control' but why? I thought this was very odd, after all isn't it normal to want to move when you hear music? Maybe not for all, but certainly not a sign of bad behaviour surely.

Believing that it would be wonderful if governments could also celebrate and measure the success of schools based not mainly on academia but also on singing, dancing, socialisation, art, performance, sport, kindness and tolerance; to include all varying talents, such as kind and considerate pupils who have advanced communicative skills, achievements, talent competitions of all kinds and inventions. This is not an exhaustive list. Currently the most dominant measure as to whether the school is 'Outstanding' or 'Good' still rests on the main point of academic results in relation to grades achieved in Maths, English, and Science.

Naturally, the school concentrates most of their efforts in these areas, and as we know some schools are better at ensuring that activities for wellbeing are still very much in place, as even the teachers know that without them we do not grow well-rounded and happy children prepared for adult life.

These pressures in our mainstream education system not only create environments where teachers are closely scrutinised, but they are rewarded for good performance. So if the performance is directly linked to grades, a teacher will be left with the dilemma of wanting to help all pupils fairly, however they know that for their personal benefits they will need to concentrate on the pupils that will achieve the best grades for them. I'm sure most teachers entered into the profession to provide an education to all.

So, the question has to be asked of governments - what is the most important factor? Educating everybody to be the best they possibly can be, or being more selective about higher grades for some, therefore in some strange way to prove the public educational system does work, whilst other less academically gifted children may be passed over as a kind of hinderance, particularly in the larger classes. Surely there are much better ways to measure the competency levels of our teachers in mainstream education.

Currently as some parents know, we already have too many children with high levels of anxiety in relation to education, and we have to ask the question – is this really what we want for our children? Sleepless nights for any child creates family heartache, let alone very young children having sleepless nights worrying about a test the next day.

Surely this is not what any parent wanted when they first looked into their new-born's eyes. Even worse to be told they need medication to concentrate as this just makes the parents and child feel incredibly inadequate at such an innocent and young age. Is this really the education system necessary to gear our kids up for the big wide world?

Not all children will become doctors, lawyers, or scientists. We really should be celebrating the differences of our children, as this is what in turn will make our economies strong. Having creative ideas with well thought out business solutions, backed with the confidence to put them forward, and of course never fearing failure, because everybody has to fail to become great.

When a child loses self-belief in their abilities, it destroys self-esteem. Our system can be ruthless in the way in which it can negatively brand and categorise children using stereotypical criteria to measure what 'clever' and 'bright' looks like.

We live in a world of critics and opinions of what is right and wrong, what looks good or not, and who should be popular and who should not.

Staggeringly, more and more children are struggling with mental health conditions that can change the course of their future and lives forever.

The definition of mental health illness is *'a condition which causes serious disorder in a person's behaviour or thinking.'*

In 2017, the NHS published figures stating that one in eight people in England under the age of 19 had a disorder. The study found that of 9,117 children and young people surveyed, the incidence of disorders rose to one in six between people aged 17 to 19.

Boys were found to be more likely to have a mental health disorder than girls until the age of 11. Between 11 and 16 years, both genders were equally likely to have mental health issues, but by the time they reached 17 to 19, girls were more than twice as likely to be suffering with their mental health.

Within this age range, almost one in four girls had a mental health disorder of some description, with more than half admitting that they had self-harmed, and considered or even attempted suicide.

Interestingly, the NHS survey also included pre-school children for the first time, where mental health disorders were found to be one in eighteen. Within this age group, boys were more than 50% more likely to have a disorder than girls.

So, what happens as our children are growing up?

Of course, we cannot apportion blame to the education system as a whole. However, there must be more that can be done during our children's educational journey to build self-worth and self-esteem. We need to provide them with better tool kits that help them recognise their own self-worth, and also importantly respect that in those around them.

Along with a shortage of teachers, performance-related pay, and bonus systems to encourage academic achievement in schools, whilst reducing stimulating subjects such as music, art and sport to replace them with the more academic subjects, in an attempt to meet the stretching governmental targets set, are often written by people who have never worked in organisations outside of education.

It is time to wake up the system to recognise that the way in which we are educating our children is old fashioned and has had its day. That day being 'the Industrial Revolution'.

The facts are that whilst we continue to adopt antiquated teaching methods and measures with the 'old school' mentality, we will always have children who are worried, anxious, or even worse, suffering with their mental health. Surely, with the experiences so many children, parents and their wider families have, we should all be questioning:

'What is our education system there to achieve?'

and hoping to get the answer

'Well grounded, talented, confident individuals who feel great about who they are, with the confidence to go and get a job or career suitable for their personal talents and aspirations.'

Whoever you are and wherever you live, most of us need to know where we fit in; feel a sense of belonging, a sense of acceptance and almost more importantly, that we are contributing to someone or something.

Everybody needs a purpose in life!

It is no different for the younger generations. They also need to know how they fit into the jigsaw, how they solve the puzzle, what they bring to the table. In turn they then learn:

Self-respect - Self-love - Self-motivation!

This book is entitled *'Unbrand My Child'* and I hope you'll join me in supporting the need for our system to adapt, evolve and change to ensure all our children's strengths are enhanced and their needs are supported.

The 'branding' system currently used in education to categorise children, teenagers and young adults into bundles should be revisited with fresh eyes and with practical, real life examples of what success looks like for all talents and all children.

As I strongly believe that all children are special, if we grow their unique talents, we will grow healthy, well-balanced adults who know their own self-worth and in turn feel confident to contribute amazing things to the world they live in.

> *"The things that make me different*
> *are the things that make me, me..."*

Piglet

Light Bulb Activity

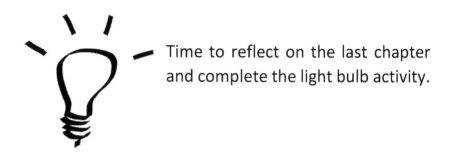 Time to reflect on the last chapter and complete the light bulb activity.

What was interesting in the last chapter?

How can this knowledge be used to your advantage?

Where and when can you implement any new ideas or plans to help with this?

Chapter Two

Food for Thought

"I failed in some subjects in exams,
but my friend passed in all.
Now he is an engineer for Microsoft
and I am the owner of Microsoft."

Bill Gates

In 2004, Cass; one of Europe's leading busines schools based in London published a press release with the headline *"Entrepreneurs five times more likely to suffer from dyslexia"*. Its subheading went on to ask, *"What makes Sir Richard Branson, Sir Alan Sugar and Sir Norman*

Foster special?", which is also the first sentence in the Preface from the acclaimed book *'The Dyslexic Advantage'* by Dr Brock L. Eide and Dr Fernette F Eide.

In addition, a world leader in professional development American Management Association (AMA) who are known for advancing the skills of individuals to drive business success by having an approach to improving performance, combining experiential learning – *'learning through doing'* - with opportunities for ongoing professional growth at every step of one's career journey. They support the goals of individuals and organisations through a complete range of products and services, including seminars, webcasts and podcasts, conferences, corporate and government solutions, business books and research.

In 2019 they published research which found that a staggering 35% of US entrepreneurs suffer from dyslexia, compared to 20% in the UK, according to a new study by Julie Logan, Professor of Entrepreneurship at London's Cass Business School.

The US study follows up earlier research which revealed that UK entrepreneurs are five times more likely to suffer from dyslexia than the average UK citizen (4% of the general UK population is dyslexic). In the US, dyslexia is grouped under a 'learning disabled' umbrella, which includes 15% of the population.

Some examples of dyslexic entrepreneurs are: Kinko's founder Paul Orfalea, Jupiter Media CEO Alan Meckler, and legendary investor Charles Schwab.

Many entrepreneurs cite good communication as a key factor in their success. *"Entrepreneurs are masters at communicating with their team, their customers and the media. They have a clear, uncomplicated style of communication that wins hearts and minds"*, says Professor Logan. Her study showed that while dyslexic entrepreneurs seemed on a par with their non-dyslexic counterparts in terms of attributes such as vision and determination, stating that *"There was a trend for dyslexics to perceive themselves as being better at communication."*

Key findings from Professor Logan's research showed that dyslexics are more likely than non-dyslexics to:

Own more than one business.

Run their businesses for a shorter time (although grow them more quickly).

Start their businesses right after school.

Excel in oral communications, problem solving, delegation, and spatial awareness.

Be influenced by a mentor (vs. non-dyslexics, who are more influenced by educational experiences).

Manage more staff (25 as mean [average] vs. 17 for non-dyslexics) because of increased ability to delegate (an example of a coping strategy employed to overcome difficulties).

Professor Logan says the primary reason why the US has a greater number of dyslexic entrepreneurs than the UK is because America has better systems for identification, intervention, and support of those with dyslexia at a young age, giving them a much better chance of success. She states, *"The UK system fails to identify dyslexics at a young age, meaning that many of those with potential to be successful entrepreneurs never get the chance. We should be producing more Richard Bransons, but the system is failing our children."*

The study reveals that while both US and UK school systems fail dyslexics in helping them to achieve academically, dyslexic entrepreneurs in the US say they enjoyed their academic experience. Their UK counterparts report having had a generally negative experience. Professor Logan said a major contributing reason for this difference in attitude is that the general teaching styles adopted in the UK - lectures and case studies - are a struggle for dyslexics. Other major problems in the UK are the absence of a standard system for identifying dyslexic pupils and a lack of awareness of the condition by teachers.

Additional findings

Those studied in the US had a high degree of self-confidence compared with low self-confidence amongst their UK counterparts.

The education systems in the UK and US are set up in such a way that they discourage achievement among the most innovative students.

The US has better systems in place to identify innovative students and provide support to help them succeed.

In the US dyslexics are teamed up with mentors at a young age—a highly effective way of helping them achieve.

The US has better programmes and greater resources to aid dyslexic children.

For further information about Professor Logan's study, visit: www.cass.city.ac.uk

The list can go on and on as to why we should be revisiting our education system.

The following letter was sent from a teacher to her pupils to ensure the pupils realised they were 'amazing' in their own way.

"Dear X

I am writing to congratulate you on your success that has come from your exceptional behaviour and approach to learning during year 6, it has been an absolute pleasure to teach you. Your energy and fun character means you always bring a smile to everybody's face and you enhance everyday with your creative imagination and kind heart.

As you know, school tests only measure a very small part of who you are and your abilities far outweigh these measures. You have amazing artistic talents, you always care for other people and your beautiful singing voice brightens up the dullest days in the classroom. You take part in sports and always give 100% to your teammates and your ability to interact and communicate with everybody far outweigh any qualification that you may gain from your SATs.

In life these attributes will go a long way to ensuring you will be successful in everything you do, so well done for being such a beautiful well-rounded individual.

Well done! We and your parents are very proud of you.

Best wishes

Mrs Steel"

How many parents would value receiving a letter like this? The question that should also be asked is *'Why does a teacher feel the need to write such a letter?'*

"The fact is that given the challenges we face, education doesn't need to be reformed - it needs to be transformed. The key to this transformation is not to standardize education, but to personalize it, to build achievement on discovering the individual talents of each child, to put students in an environment where they want to learn and where they can naturally discover their true passions."

Sir Ken Robinson

In the United Kingdom, Ofsted inspections were established in 1993 to provide a *'comprehensive and impartial picture of how well a school is performing.'*

Many other countries also have similar governing bodies in place.

It's always interesting to read reports from the governing bodies, and the grading they provide of each school.

YouGov conducted a *'Teacher Attitude Survey'* in 2019 name teachers' awareness and perceptions of Ofsted.

There were some interesting results reported back by teachers.

The following extracts are cited from the YouGov's findings:

'Overall opinion of Ofsted has fallen since last year. Agreement that Ofsted acts as a reliable and trusted arbiter has fallen from 35% in 2018 to 18% this year. But, for the most part, teachers are not more likely to disagree but to choose neither agree nor disagree. Those who were most recently inspected were less likely to disagree than those who were inspected one to two years ago.'

'Only 27% of teachers feel inspections help individual schools improve (27% compared with 31% in 2018) but there has been an increase in perception that Ofsted inspectors have relevant frontline experience.'

'41% of teachers currently feel that their school places a greater emphasis on getting good results than the content of the learning. This is significantly higher than parents' perception, which shows 24% feel this. Of those who work in a school that places a greater emphasis on getting good results than the content of the learning, seven in ten (70%) teachers disagree with this focus being taken in their school.'

'Half (51%) of teachers still think that an Ofsted inspection means doing extra and unnecessary work.'

'Teachers who agree that inspections are important and necessary has fallen from 50% to 38% over the last year. This is largely due to an increase in teachers stating 'neither agree nor disagree.'

So, amongst many findings in 2019, it is interesting that 62% of our teachers neither agree nor disagree that inspections are necessary or important, a very worrying statistic since our teachers are the people at the frontline and thus must know what works and what is not working.

Although from the analysis it is not entirely clear as to what teachers would change in relation to the governing body, it is clear further questions would be beneficial.

As most people would agree, Governing bodies in education play a vitally important role, providing they are measuring the right things. We, as in many other countries, are driven by politics in our education system and this in turn means that the system is constantly being changed to fulfil the latest government guidelines. The knock-on effect to schools can only be dramatic changes every time, not only in the curriculum but also behaviours and cultures within the schools themselves.

The UK education system follows the STEM subjects, which stands for Science, Technology, Engineering and Maths, and include Biology, Chemistry, Physics, Design and Technology (D&T), Maths, Economics, Geography and

Computer Science, Information and/or Communications Technology (IT or ICT).

Subjects such as Physical Education are still compulsory, however the guidelines are a minimum of 2 hours per week.

Over many years, I have trained thousands of people in companies and organisations and equal numbers of successful business leaders. Leaders who have followed the academic route of college or university and many that have not. All of whom bring fantastic ideas and solutions to the Boardroom table, and all who, fortunately, think very differently.

One common thread that all successful businesses and organisations know is that diverse thinking is critical, particularly in times of great economic challenge and uncertainty, such as during the COVID-19 pandemic.

The great thing about children is that they are unique, and in order to learn they have to get things wrong. To them, it is a level playing field, learning is fun and making mistakes is absolutely normal. In fact, I'd go as far as to say, an important part of their development.

When a child starts to crawl, the next stage is to stand up and the next stage is to walk, however the common obstacles in this development pattern is that they will inevitably fail the first few times until they learn how to balance and navigate their path. In this example, we are generally encouraging and supportive to ensure the child feels positive about the whole experience. This point of failing and then picking themselves up, does not change in life in any development situation.

The important part of this is that it is vitally important that children feel and believe their carers, parents and guardians are not prejudging or criticising them unnecessarily. Children need to know they are accepted as 'normal' how they are, in the rawest sense of the word.

Every living person has an inbuilt mechanism for survival, often referred to the 'fight and flight' system and when that is threatened, quite naturally, we trigger innate behaviours which enable us to survive. Whether this is physical or mental threats, children naturally develop coping mechanisms.

Some attitudes in these situations will create positive behaviours of resilience and stamina, however at times unfortunately some more negative behaviours will create rebellion and defiance. All very natural reactions to ensuring we survive the ups and downs of life.

Of course, for children that have strong talents for logic and linguistics in the current education system they should be able to flourish. However, the downside is that as our State education system has been designed elevating some subjects over others, such as English,

Grammar and Maths, this for too many children may be very challenging, particularly when being taught in very large groups or classes. Along with the fact that as we are unique, we learn in different ways.

This means that some children who have a tendency to learn well when watching and listening, will flourish in a traditional classroom or lecture environment. However, for some children who learn better in experiential and physical environments, this can be stifling in their early years and unfortunately can completely turn them off education and learning, having a knock-on effect into later life.

Although I strongly believe that many attributes can be built from challenges we experience in our lives, I also believe that by elevating the less considered or favoured subjects and developing physical environments to deliver them, we could build greater self-esteem in our children.

Having much higher levels of positive interaction would, in turn, result in happier students and far less behavioural issues, including bullying, in our school playgrounds.

Because we negatively brand some subjects as being for the less clever students, we condition and drive negative behaviours towards all groups, including pupils that are talented academically, physically, creatively, musically and the list goes on.

Negative branding is too frequently damaging for so many and this is an important topic that should be investigated with a view to finding solutions.

The following information was taken from The National Mental Health Development Unit (NMHDU), a Government agency charged with supporting the implementation of mental health policy in England by the Department of Health in collaboration with the NHS, Local Authorities, and other major stakeholders. (DH Gateway ref: 14559)

'The financial costs of the adverse effects of mental illness on people's quality of life are estimated at £41.8 billion per annum in England. Wider costs to the national economy in terms of welfare benefits, lost productivity at work etc. amount to some £77 billion a year.'

PREVALENCE OF MENTAL HEALTH CONDITIONS

One in six adults will have a mental health problem at any one time.

17.6% of adults in England have at least one common mental disorder.

0.4% of adults in England have a psychotic disorder, and 80% are receiving treatment.

0.3% of adults in England have antisocial personality disorder.

0.4% of adults in England have borderline personality disorder.

10% of children in the UK have a diagnosable mental health condition.

13–16% of older people in England have severe depression, and up to 50% of older people are in residential care.

One in twenty people over 65 in the UK have some form of dementia, rising to one in five people over 80.

One third of all mental health service activity in England is concerned with the care and treatment of people over 65.

All these statistics are staggering, and we need to see what else can be done at an early age to help prevent some of these terrible illnesses. All children grow up to be adults and the more coping mechanism they have for life, the better equipped they will be to cope throughout their lives.

Although I am not suggesting for one moment that we can eradicate mental illness, or associated conditions, I am challenging why we are not considering the impacts on negative branding through education on mental wellbeing.

In other words, measuring schools on how well integrated all pupils are and how they feel instead of endless measures on whether a child, at the age of ten, can spell words such as *fabulously, sabotaging, xenobiotic, dalmatians, gallamines* creating problems such as dyslexia. Although I am not undermining the need to spell, the levels we expect at such early ages far outweigh our current measures for having fun, being happy and having a strong sense of self-worth.

Interestingly, **Nick Gibb was appointed Minister of State at the Department for Education on 15 July 2014.**

Just days after being appointed as Minister for Schools in 2010, Gibb was criticised after leaked information suggested he had told officials at the Department of Education that he *"would rather have a physics graduate from Oxbridge without a PGCE teaching in a school than a physics graduate from one of the rubbish universities with a PGCE."*

In October 2015, Nick Gibb published his view on education and in particular Maths and English, some of which is cited below:

"Maths and English are both crucial subjects needed to get on in life whether through employment or further study. It is therefore essential that a world-class, academically rigorous curriculum reflects this and supports all pupils in

their study both pre- and post-GCSE for those that do achieve a grade C and for those that don't."

Comparing our education and results with Shanghai, Gibb proceeded to make changes in the way we teach Maths and English in schools to improve grades. Although there is absolutely nothing wrong with wanting to improve grades, it is vitally important to consider other factors that can be affected when we make changes.

In Gibb's opinion, he thought that the curriculum prioritised inefficient methods in Maths with an over-emphasis on concepts such as 'learning to learn' and 'individualised instruction' at the expense of content, practice and, through that, fluency and mastery.

At the time, in the UK, 38% of 19-year-olds left full time education failing to achieve A* - C in English and Maths.

He set out to reform the curriculum at secondary level education to make it more challenging. He stated that Maths GCSE will contain broader and deeper mathematical content which requires more teaching time, greater fluency, and deeper understanding. A-levels will see the introduction of only a small amount of new content, but, again, with the requirement for deeper understanding.

This will exist alongside the new Core Maths qualifications for those who do achieve a C or better at GCSE but who elect not to go on to A-level.

On the 22nd August 2019, the Government published a review of results for 2017-2019 entitled:

Variability in GCSE results for schools and colleges 2017-2019.

Analysis of how GCSE results for schools and colleges have changed in recent years.

The main findings were as follows:

- In general, the level of variation in individual school and college results at grades 9 to 4 or A* to C is slightly less than in previous years.
- Differences between the average (mean) percentage of students achieving grades 9 to 4 or A* to C 2018/2019 and in 2017/2018 are generally small, indicating that year-on-year results in the subjects analysed have remained relatively stable.
- Even when there are no changes to qualifications, individual schools and colleges will see variation in their year-on-year results: this is normal.

So, in essence, the changes made have clearly not been reflective in the grades, yet the upheaval for schools and pupils to adapt to these changes would have been huge.

Schools should be places where pupils are safe and happy and in order to ensure this they must have fun and be able to enjoy physical activities, have a sense of belonging and being accepted, knowing people believe in them and that they are culturally accepted.

And if they are struggling in any of these areas, they need somebody to go to. A person that will not judge them regardless.

Currently the United Kingdom's National Curriculum for pages given to subjects is shown below in the Bar chart.

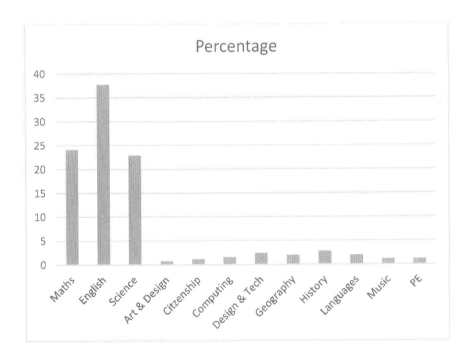

This clearly displays that the majority of the document is detailing expected level of criteria for Maths, English, and Science with a total of 160 pages from a 200-page document. All other subjects are allocated just 40 pages. No wonder our learners are becoming switched off.

Surely it makes sense to build the top three subjects into the other subjects to create more stimulation for learning, such as Maths into physical lessons and woodwork classes and English into History and Geography for example. Instead these subjects are reduced to allow for such a ridiculously level of grammar for a ten-year-old.

In fact, the situation has got to a stage where Leo Winkley the Headmaster of a well-known independent school in Shrewsbury, recently wrote to the Telegraph as follows:

'Sir – After a summer of examination results carnage, it is timely to challenge the fitness for purpose of GCSEs.

Written examinations are not the only way to assess pupils' learning; nor do they recognise the aptitudes and skills that parents, educators and employers more obviously value.

A crisis of confidence in the examination system affords a real opportunity to reinvent the way we measure personal development.

Examinations are generally felt to be the fairest way to judge the extent to which content has been consumed and can then be regurgitated. Yet any adult would concede that readiness for life is much more than the ability to complete written tests.

Surely human ingenuity can devise ways to recognise the role of character, social skills and collaboration in enhanced life chances.

Why not put more faith in teachers to assess a wide scorecard of aptitudes, rather than a battery of written assessments? Real life is much less controlled than an exam hall.

Of course, there is a need for the assessment of knowledge gained and progress made. This could be better achieved through a blend of written tests, diagnostic interviews and practical problem-solving scenarios that assess the application of learning.'

Incidentally, Shrewsbury School recently won the Independent School of the Year 2020 at a virtual national awards ceremony held on 8th October 2020, and although I think it would be unwise to leave the grading of a student purely to teachers, overall Leo Winkley makes a very strong point that deserves the right to be explored in relation to the way our examination process operates.

Schools should be a place for enjoyment, safety and learning where we build self-esteem and well-balanced pupils. I remember when I was at primary school, my buddy was a very kind dinner lady called Mrs Smith, a well-balanced, warm lady with a bright face and huge smile. All the children would go to her for comfort and daily chats. These characters in our schools are critical for our children's happiness and education of how to behave in the big world. Never being judged on what happens the day before, who fell out with who, and certainly not how clever, or not, in the eyes of the education system you are.

Everybody is accepted and every child's feelings about who they are is vitally important to helping them be happy.

A teacher is a person who teaches, usually their vocation at a school or similar academic institution. However, what makes a teacher a 'GREAT' teacher?

Think of your favourite teacher at school and why you remember them in such a positive way? Maybe it was because they were enthusiastic or passionate, particularly knowledgeable about their subject(s) or just seemed really happy in their role? Was it because you felt or thought that they cared for YOU and your education on an individual level? The facts remain, that being a 'great teacher' is an absolute skill set in its own right.

Another definition of a great teacher might be...

Someone who can freely teach with enthusiasm and the children learn without realising they have been learning. One who genuinely cares about the kids and treats them fairly and equally, even the 'bad' ones.

Light Bulb Activity

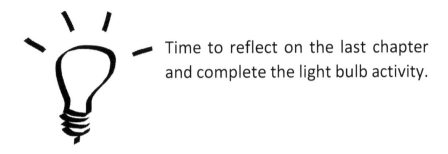 Time to reflect on the last chapter and complete the light bulb activity.

What was interesting in the last chapter?

How can this knowledge be used to your advantage?

Where and when can you implement any new ideas or plans to help with this?

Chapter Three

You Belong Here

"School was a struggle for me, people just thought I was thick. I really needed someone to help me and understand my strengths."

Jamie Oliver

Most people need to feel they belong somewhere and that they fit in to their environment. In school we all know, particularly since the outbreak of the COVID-19 pandemic and resultant school closures, that friendships are so important for a child's happiness. When they do not have this interaction with their schoolfriends, it can have varying levels of emotional impact and this is absolutely normal behaviour for most children.

Acceptance is critical from the moment we are born and enables us to develop a content and happy mind. When our children are young, we as parents are generally quick to ensure we join groups, mix with friends and family, so that our children can interact with other individuals of a similar age. This ensures that they gain the essential social skills they require to grow into well-balanced adults and there has been endless amounts of research to prove how important this is for childhood development and social skills.

School plays a critical role in ensuring children feel safe, believe they belong there, and that they have something to give to the world they live in. When we categorise them into different groups, we send a message to them that they are different. For some, this transfers a positive message that they are gifted and bright, however for others, it may be interpreted that they are not so clever, nor bright which sometimes makes them feel they fit into a 'special' category. Some may even view this as not being normal, although of course they are absolutely normal, and the label can be extremely negative for them.

So, let us think about that message we are sending to all pupils. You are either bright and gifted or you are not, so need extra help. Neither category is perfect, as segregation can only mean differences, which is something we are striving to avoid in our societies and certainly in every business. So why do we allow this to happen in our schools?

As we will explore later in this book, with unique approaches and talents come brilliant ideas and often solutions. Thinking differently and creatively can solve many puzzles. We are all unique and different, and those differences enable us to think and behave in ways that solutions can be sought to problems.

Many organisations search for varying talents, as they know it will make their proposition stronger and often diverse thinking creates great solutions to challenges.

The difficulty is that differences are frequently perceived by others to be a problem or a learning disadvantage, which is negative. Moreover, this is often not true. With adaptions to the traditional way in which classes are taught, we can easily remedy some learning differences.

Separating and highlighting certain pupils by removing them from lessons to partake in 'special' activities simply just highlights to the child, and their peers, that they are 'different'.

Of course, these are challenges for mainstream schools, however the emotional impacts of this can be very damaging for a child's self-esteem and in some cases, make them negatively stand out from the crowd.

Segregation of this type, without a doubt, creates repercussions in personal behaviour and can forge the foundations of disruptive mannerism or even worse, bullying.

The most negative message we can send to children is that they are different, and that this difference is not an advantage. This is where the term 'special needs' rings out negatively for too many children, as well as their parents. The label does not create anything positive, except that finally the child may get some extra help in class to meet the grades required by the governing bodies.

Diversifying from the common way of teaching in an educational system that is already overstretched from a resourcing perspective would be such a huge task. Instead schools are forced to follow stringent government measures, which create fantastic academics, however the system has not considered that many industries do not need academics. So, although they are a valuable resource, they are not the only resource needed.

Maybe it is because the governments fear that if the education system was changed to enable it to create diversity and build on individual needs it would just overstretch the schooling system further. Although I would argue this would save huge amounts in the long-term in relation to the economy and other strains on governments as a result of a dysfunctional system.

One thing is for sure, as long as we accept it, we will always have struggling children who should not need to struggle, nor feel so different to others. Worse still, we will create a breeding ground for hierarchical bullying due to conditioning our children to believe some are better than others. And bullying can happen either way. Meaning we are encouraging bullying in our schools because we make children feel good or bad depending on their educational abilities outlined by governments.

We may hear phrases about 'teamwork' and 'group activities', however for teams to achieve well, they not only need a common goal – they need different talents.

High achievement is gained from varying approaches and attributes that are working collaboratively together. If we put this into the big world of grown-ups, an example would be that success comes from a company working together across all skill sets, such as sales, marketing, finance, operations, research and design, production, quality control, distribution. All which have different people with a diverse range of skills and competencies and often poles apart, yet all add value to the common goal and result.

Let's consider an extremely successful Company called ABC Limited. Why are they successful? Because they employ a very talented and diverse team of people who collectively provide fantastic products and services for their customers.

Rupinder, the accountant, is extremely analytical with great attention to detail along with his ability to stay focussed on the job in hand. Whilst others in the office are drawn into banter and discussions, Rupinder keeps his head down and gets on with his work. He is not great with customers, however there are lots of other people there to take care of that.

Sophie is the Sales Director and a great leader of people. She has a big personality, very positive and energetic and relies on Rupinder to work out his projections and figures to quote to customers. Being a people person, Sophie at times lacks attention to detail, but then Rupinder takes care of that. Sophie is great at building strong relationships with her customers, and when she does not know the answer she gets the information from the rest of her team.

Mark works the complicated 3D laser cutter, and he loves innovation and learning how new things work. Most of all he is very creative with new product development and designs. He is not really a people person and is more interested in coming up with new ideas than looking at small amounts of details. Mark is dyslexic so relies on Marissa to write up the product descriptions for him.

Marissa is the Office Manager and looks after everyone and everything. She is extremely caring and considered a bit of a parent figure for the whole team. People always go to Marissa when they need a friendly face to talk to. She can also do many jobs, but she is not much of an expert, more of an all-rounder. Marissa always knows where to go to get a job sorted if need be.

Jackie, in the Warehouse, looks after despatch. She is considered by most to be the Company's hardest working employee as she arrives first thing to arrange deliveries and can load into a lorry 100 boxes per hour. She has a great sense of humour and is not phased when things go wrong. She knows how to work all the equipment, including the forklift truck and can drive the lorries. She always knows exactly where everything is in the warehouse. Jackie left school at 16 as she was disruptive in class so did not manage to get any qualifications. Working by herself in the warehouse gives her a strong sense of achievement and she is respected by everyone as a reliable member of the team who never moans (even when the warehouse is freezing cold) and always goes the extra mile.

Finally, Winston is ABC Limited's Managing Director. He left school with virtually no qualifications and during his education, lacked concentration and focus in any one area at a time. Someone whose mind always wanders, Winston's always coming up with new ideas and pushing boundaries as to what is possible. Upon leaving school Winston decided he was probably unemployable and for this reason set up ABC Limited at the age of 18. Winston recognises that in business, the sum of the equal parts is greater than the whole.

Each individual in ABC Company has a very different set of skills and competency levels, however each member is equally talented and respected for their contribution to the Company, all important cogs in the wheel.

We can all see how ABC Company works in industry, so why does the education system only elevate Rupinder in accountancy skills and not the rest of the team? Incidentally, all but Rupinder, were deemed by the education system as failures.

Childhood is such a critical time for the development of behaviour, self-belief, and esteem. There has been so much research into mindfulness, positive mental attitude and wellbeing, and, as adults, we have access to hundreds of self-help books.

If an adult joined a company, the organisation would make the necessary adjustments to ensure the employee was not treated differently or with any prejudice. Purely because successful organisations know that diversity amongst their workforce and the talents, ideas, and approaches their people possess, ensures that they can healthily grow and expand their businesses.

As already discussed, education is so important and the ability for children to learn how to read and write fluently, as well as practice mental arithmetic is imperative. However, it's arguably as important to instil self-belief and mindfulness into our children during their formative years. Living for the moment and enjoying the day with as little anxiety as possible surely safeguards that they grow up believing they are great in their own individual ways, and most importantly, that they can add value somewhere. Afterall, life events outside our control may create anxieties, however our children should definitely not be experiencing high levels of stress because our schooling system is antiquated in the way in which it is set up and governed.

Everybody, whether a child or an adult needs a sense of belonging and attachment to someone or something. It is generally something that makes the person feel good about who they are or provides a sense of being part of something. As we know, this can be negative for some people, however human desire is to know where you fit in.

Everybody needs to know where they add value to society and communities, and as importantly the need to be proud of what they contribute.

We are at risk of losing our sense of where adolescents feel they contribute and add value and we are conditioned to undervalue the other talents people may have. Creativity, empathy, communication, art, nature, cookery, all the other things that show great talents, yet are categorised as hobby type vocations, rather than something that the person can do and do really well.

So, to recap, school has a critical role to play in making sure everybody fits in, that everyone belongs there and that everybody feels safe. This is, without a doubt, what our education system should be striving to achieve, along with the subjects necessary to ensure they can attain their goals and dreams to be great in their chosen careers as adults.

Light Bulb Activity

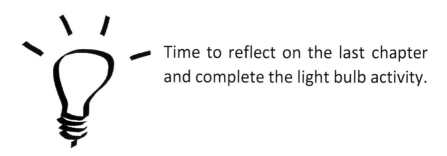

Time to reflect on the last chapter and complete the light bulb activity.

What was interesting in the last chapter?

How can this knowledge be used to your advantage?

Where and when can you implement any new ideas or plans to help with this?

Chapter Four

Motivation

*"Human resources are like natural resources;
they're often buried deep.
You have to go looking for them,
they're not just lying around on the surface.
You have to create the circumstances
where they show themselves."*

Sir Ken Robinson

Motivation is such an interesting and in-depth subject and each of us have different motivators and ideas of success.

Research has shown that we have two types of motivation: Intrinsic Motivation and Extrinsic Motivation.

So, what are the differences between them? Intrinsic Motivation comes from within, whereas Extrinsic is derived from external influences.

To explore further, Intrinsic Motivation is when somebody is motivated to carry out an activity because they personally enjoy it. It is completely for personal gain and does not carry a reward other than of personal satisfaction, such as a hobby or interest. Other examples would be participating in a sport because you find the activity enjoyable, cleaning your room because you like tidying up, solving a puzzle because you find the challenge fun, learning about a subject because you find it interesting.

Extrinsic Motivation is about external gains, such as being acknowledged as the best by others, possibly receiving financial rewards, and recognition in awards. Some examples would be participating in a sport to win the tournament and a trophy, cleaning your room to avoid being reprimanded by your parents, competing in a contest to win a scholarship, learning about a subject because you want to get a good marks.

If we think about Intrinsic Motivation as a self-motivator and Extrinsic as an external motivator, it generally follows that Intrinsic is the most positive as the motivation is driven from the energy of enjoyment and enthusiasm. However, we cannot always rely on Intrinsic Motivation, so Extrinsic Motivation is sometimes used. However, it is always wise to understand when you are using either one as personal goals and drivers for achievement which are often more positive than enforcing penalties to motivate an individual.

So, if you want somebody to carry out an activity or task, generally it is best for them to understand the personal benefits that achieving the task will bring, rather than threatening consequences if the task is not achieved. An example of this is when a child is reading a book they enjoy and gain satisfaction from, rather than being forced to read about a subject they have no interest in. If the original goal is to teach the child how to read, then allowing them to read a book they enjoy and choose themselves will appeal to them personally. This is Intrinsic Motivation.

It is professionally researched that Intrinsic and Extrinsic motivation play a significant role in learning. Some experts argue that the traditional emphasis on external rewards such as grades, reports, head teacher awards and house points undermine any existing Intrinsic Motivation that students might have. However, others suggest that these Extrinsic Motivators help leaners feel more competent in the classroom, thus enhancing Intrinsic Motivation.

The main points are that balance is critical here. If we only concentrate on Extrinsic Motivators, naturally the learners who find the subject matter challenging will struggle to achieve high levels in that subject and may become demotivated very quickly.

However, it is also recognised that if learners do benefit from Extrinsic rewards, we must always understand the Intrinsic purpose of learning a given subject. So therefore, it is important to contextualise subject matters that we teach, ensuring the learner sees it as relevant, along with making the learning enjoyable and stimulating for the brain.

If we pay attention to the emotional wellbeing of a child such as friendship groups, a sense of belonging, being accepted, feeling safe, as well as reaping the rewards for good behaviour, hard work and grades – then will we truly feed the basic needs that we have as humans and reduce the endless examples we have of children with anxiety and mental health issues due to unnecessary stress levels.

Notice should also be given to Abraham Maslow research into motivation shown in the model as the Hierarchy of Needs.

This model shows us that the first level of motivation is the need for 'Physiological' items which are basic things we need to survive such as food, water, shelter, sleep, and reproduction.

Maslow's Hierarchy of Needs

Self Actualisation
desire to become the most that one can be

Esteem
respect, self esteem, status, recognition, strength, freedom

Love and Belonging
friendship, intimacy, family, sense of connection

Safety Needs
personal secuirty, employment, resources, health, property

Physiological Needs
air, water, food, shelter, sleep, clothing, reproduction

It then follows that second basic level is our strong need for 'Safety'. Feeling safe, secure, and healthy applies to both home, school, and any other environment that the child may find themselves. So, for a child that feels that they 'don't fit in' or even worse, feels bullied, the second level is not met, which in turn means they will struggle to climb to the next level in Maslow's Hierarchy.

Providing the basic levels of 'Physiological' and 'Safety' are achieved, the next level is a psychological level known as 'Love and Belonging'. As per the previous chapter, everybody has a need to know that they belong to something, they deserve to be there, and that they are accepted. So, for a person who does not think they are clever enough, or they feel worthless and have nothing to add to the environment they find themselves in, this need cannot be met.

Again, although this is challenging in the current system, we must always strive as an educator to ensure everybody feels they fit in and has something to bring to the table. If they don't, the knock-on effects will be negative and naturally, we may see disengagement of the learner.

This disengagement can be displayed in the individual's behaviour by them not applying themselves to the lesson being taught and at times the teacher, or possibly in them being disruptive throughout the learning. Either are not good for the individual, the other classmates, or the teacher.

When the first three levels of Maslow's Hierarchy have been met the individual can reach the next psychological level of 'Esteem' needs. It is vital for an individual to feel respected and recognised as adding value, and this is also vitally important for Intrinsic and Extrinsic motivation.

The final state is 'Self-actualisation' and is the highest level of psychological development, where the 'actualisation' of full personal potential is achieved, something that only occurs after the basic and mental needs have been fulfilled. This is the stage when the individual's desires are to become the best they can be.

In context, all levels of Maslow's Hierarchy of Needs are so critical to the wellbeing and motivation of a child, and certainly to their application in the learning environment. However, in education the sense of belonging is one that I think can all too often be forgotten. If a child feels they are not up to a subject, they will feel they do not belong and the effect this has can only be negative. We all have a need to survive, and survival is about fulfilling our human needs.

In the big world this naturally manifests itself with other issues. If a young person does not know how they fit in or belong, it may result in rebellion or set them on a path to fulfil that need. If the solution is not easy to find through support and mechanisms such as education, they may wander to unsavoury places to find their sense of belonging such as groups or gangs, some of which will not be positive. Another result may be where a child becomes almost reclusive, as they do not feel they fit in, spending endless hours wandering around with no friends to attach themselves to.

Whatever the results, education should play a huge part in making sure that this does not happen, and the system should be measured accordingly. Although putting this into play within our education system would take thought and time, we must find a way to enhance other subjects, allowing children to realise how and why they add value.

All subjects should hold the same status of importance, Afterall, it is well documented that using all parts of the brain is vitally important for a happy mind.

Education should always be about creating happy and well-rounded children with the abilities to believe that they can achieve their personal goals in life, ensuring that they are confident with who they are, whilst having attainment for fulfilling their academic goals and in turn career aspirations and dreams in later life.

Whether you are brighter at English than Maths, more proficient in Food Technology than Science or more adept in Music than Sport, the same level of importance should be given to all subjects. This is the only way education is going to meet Intrinsic Motivation for all and complement all brains, which I will talk about later in this book.

So of course, the academic subjects are important but so are many others too and we need to explore how education systems can be improved by governing bodies to inject change. Change that means everybody is considered to be bright in their own way. Until we make that change, we will always have the knock-on effects of behavioural and mental health issues in our young learners.

This system would mean we celebrate everybody's talents, everyone will feel valued and in turn everybody will know they belong to something that is worthwhile.

Light Bulb Activity

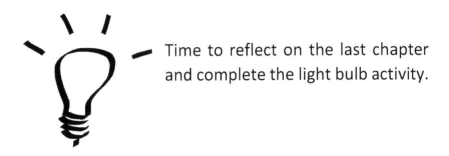

Time to reflect on the last chapter and complete the light bulb activity.

What was interesting in the last chapter?

How can this knowledge be used to your advantage?

Where and when can you implement any new ideas or plans to help with this?

Chapter Five

Wellbeing and Motivation Activity

Take the Motivation Questionnaire

The following activity has been designed for school learners to complete as a wellbeing activity. Its aim is for both children and parents to help understand what motivates them the most at school and in turn, to open up discussions in relation to 'Belonging' and 'Motivation'. This exercise is purely to explore how the learner is feeling and whether their fundamental needs are currently being met.

The activity will be more effective if the learner knows this is a supportive exercise and about the individual. It is important that they realise there are no right or wrong answers, it is purely to establish how they feel about the school environment and what is important to them personally.

It is important that the adult/parent does not try to influence the answers in any way, otherwise it is a pointless exercise.

Once the activity has been completed, please ensure you read the following notes to give guidance as to how to get the most benefit from the questionnaire.

To the person completing the activity, this is a guideline.

How to complete the activity:

- There are no right or wrong answers.
- Each line has the option of two choices from each row, please tick (only one) the choice that is of the greatest importance to you personally.
- Consistency is not important, so do not correct questions already answered.
- Complete the Questionnaire (tick only one from each line).

This activity can also be completed orally. Whereby you, (parent or guardian) verbally asks your child their preference from the two options, repeating the process 56 times.

Please select from the following:

Head Teacher Award		House Points
Good Friends		Being Trusted
Feeling Safe		Having Fun
Responsbility for a Task		Achievement Award
House Points		Having Fun
Head Teacher Award		Feeling Safe
Being Trusted		Responsbility for a Task
Good Friends		Achievement Award
Responsbility for a Task		Good Friends
House Points		Being Trusted
Achievement Award		Head Teacher Award
Feeling Safe		Being Trusted
Responsbility for a Task		House Points
Having Fun		Good Friends
Head Teacher Award		Responsbility for a Task
Achievement Award		Having Fun
Feeling Safe		House Points
Good Friends		Head Teacher Award
Being Trusted		Having Fun
Achievement Award		Feeling Safe
Having Fun		Responsbility for a Task
Head Teacher Award		Being Trusted
House Points		Good Friends
Feeling Safe		Responsbility for a Task
Head Teacher Award		Having Fun
Achievement Award		House Points
Good Friends		Feeling Safe
Being Trusted		Achievement Award
Head Teacher Award		House Points
Good Friends		Being Trusted
Feeling Safe		Having Fun

	Responsbility for a Task		Achievement Award
	House Points		Having Fun
	Head Teacher Award		Feeling Safe
	Being Trusted		Responsbility for a Task
	Good Friends		Achievement Award
	Responsbility for a Task		Good Friends
	House Points		Being Trusted
	Achievement Award		Head Teacher Award
	Feeling Safe		Being Trusted
	Responsbility for a Task		House Points
	Having Fun		Good Friends
	Head Teacher Award		Responsbility for a Task
	Achievement Award		Having Fun
	Feeling Safe		House Points
	Good Friends		Head Teacher Award
	Being Trusted		Having Fun
	Achievement Award		Feeling Safe
	Having Fun		Responsbility for a Task
	Head Teacher Award		Being Trusted
	House Points		Good Friends
	Feeling Safe		Responsbility for a Task
	Head Teacher Award		Having Fun
	Achievement Award		House Points
	Good Friends		Feeling Safe
	Being Trusted		Achievement Award

Results Tables

- Add up the number of times each choice was ticked and enter in the first column 'Sum of answers'.
- Mark in the 'Rank Order' column which characteristics you circled the largest number of times as 1st, 2nd, 3rd and so on to the 8th.
- Remember there are no right or wrong answers.

Choice	Sum of Answers	Rank Order (1-8)
Head Teacher Award		
House Points		
Good friends		
Being trusted		
Feeling Safe		
Responsibiliy for a task		
Having Fun		
Achievement Award		
Total		

The idea behind this questionnaire is to firstly understand what motivates your child the most at school and secondly, get to the root cause of any areas of concerns that your child may have.

Once you have completed the activity, consider, then answer the following sections and questions with your child.

Top Motivators

What were your top 2 or 3 choices?

Why are they the most in important to you?

How are you currently feeling in relation to the top three? (if they are being met move on to lowest section, if not continue)

What adjustments or changes can be made to make them better?

What will it mean to you if those changes are made?

How can this change be made?

What things can you do to improve this area?

What support or help do you need to improve these areas?

Lowest Motivators

From the lower list ask the following questions:

How do you feel about the motivators (if they feel okay, then the questionnaire is completed, if not then continue)?

What needs to happen to help you increase them?

What impact or benefits will this bring for you?

How can this be done?

What help or support do you need?

Agree a Plan

With your child, agree a plan of action together. It is critical at this point that the learner feels in control of what happens next and takes a lead on how to make any changes happen.

As a parent, it is always worth discussing these actions with a teacher that you trust in the school to gain some guidance and support for your child.

Light Bulb Activity

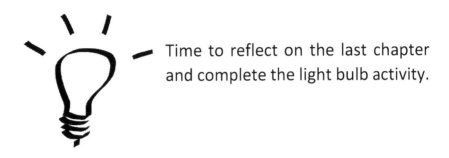 Time to reflect on the last chapter and complete the light bulb activity.

What was interesting in the last chapter?

How can this knowledge be used to your advantage?

Where and when can you implement any new ideas or plans to help with this?

Chapter Six

Multiple Intelligences and Natural Talent

*"Being dyslexic can actually help in the outside world.
I can see some things clearer than other people do
because I have to simplify things to
help me and that has helped others."*

Sir Richard Branson

Over the decades there are many accounts of extraordinarily successful, often famous characters, leaving school with little or no academic qualifications. Unfortunately, sometimes these people have been negatively branded during their education, however they have gone on to break boundaries; visionaries who pioneer innovation, build global businesses, establish institutions, represent their countries, lead nations, influence generations and, in some cases, even change the world and the course of history.

So, what is it about those people that bring them great success in their lives?

A very well-known American inventor and businessman recounted the true story from his childhood that one day he was given a letter by his teacher to take home to his mother.

Handing the letter to his mother, young Thomas watched his mother's eyes become tearful as she read the letter out loud to her child: *Your son is a genius. This school is too small for him and does not have enough good teachers for training him. Please teach him yourself.*

Many, many years later, after Thomas' mother died, and now one of the greatest inventors of the century, he was looking through old family things when he found an old, folded paper in the corner of a drawer in a desk. He took it and opened it up. On the paper was written: *"Your son is addled (def: unable to think clearly; confused). We will not let him come to school anymore."*

This was the story of Thomas Alva Edison! Described as one of the greatest inventors of all time. Amongst many achievements, he held 1,093 US patents and is credited with boasting the electric light bulb, the automatic telegraph, the movie camera, and the alkaline storage battery amongst his many inventions.

It is well cited that he cried for hours and then he wrote in his diary: *"Thomas Alva Edison was an addled child that, by a hero mother, became the genius of the century."*

Edison's life could have been far different if his mother had listened to his teacher. Edison's mother refused to accept the negative branding that was given to her young son and instead nurtured his raw talent that would go on to make him one of the most renowned inventers of all time.

His mother was remarkable, talented, and clearly extraordinarily strong. She believed in her son and so *unbranded her child*. She celebrated his uniqueness and embraced his strengths.

When we read stories like Edison's, we know they are not acceptable, and when we speak with other parents, or experience our own children being negatively branded, we should not accept this 'conditioning' that all children are born to be mathematicians, linguists or scientists experts, and if they struggle, that they are not bright!

Howard Gardner currently serves as the Chairman of Steering Committee for Project Zero at the Harvard

Graduate School of Education and is an Adjunct Professor of Psychology at Harvard University.

Having spent many years working with two vastly diverse groups; normal and gifted children, and brain-damaged adults, Gardner began developing a theory designed to synthesise his research and observations. Coined the *'Multiple Intelligences'*, Gardner published his findings in his 1983 book *'Frames of Mind'*.

According to Gardner, people have many ways of thinking and learning.

Gardner initially came up with seven Intelligences, although he said that Multiple Intelligences were not limited to the original seven, and he has since considered the existence and definitions of several other Intelligences.

For the purpose of this book, I will cover the first eight Intelligences.

Unsurprisingly, commentators and theorists continually debate and interpret potential additions to the model, and therefore you might see more than seven/eight Intelligences listed in recent interpretations of Gardner's model. The addition of Naturalist Intelligence seems most popularly considered worthy of inclusion of the potential additional Intelligences.

Gardner's Intelligences

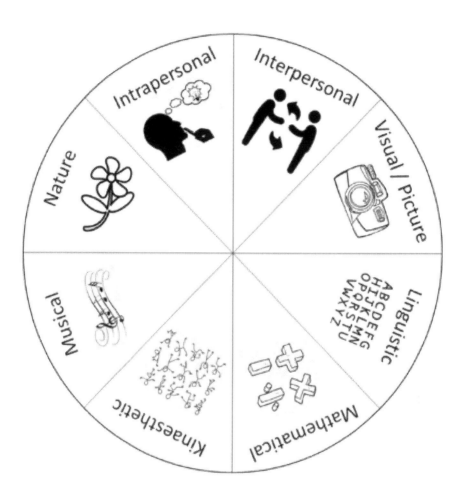

Some of the intelligence's relation to Visual and Picture, Linguistic and Verbal, Bodily Kinaesthetic, Musical, Interpersonal (the ability to understand others), Intrapersonal (the ability to understand oneself) and of course Mathematical.

Thinking about yourself, or children around you, you will be able to identify your own and that of your children's preferences.

My point is that all education and learning should be as important as a measure to whether a school is providing a well-rounded syllabus and hence, creating well-adjusted, confident and happy adults that in turn add value to organisations and/or society in later life utilising their raw talents.

When watching our children grow and develop by concentrating on what a child can do, rather than constantly on what they cannot do, must be more beneficial for their wellbeing and self-worth.

Although it is healthy for all adults to know and understand their limitations, if we concentrate most of our efforts on the areas for development, we create limiting beliefs that can become stifling as we advance in years and become adults.

Thankfully, Gardner's theory has had the greatest impact within the field of education, where it has received considerable attention and indeed, application. His conceptualisation of intelligence as more than a single, solitary quality has opened the doors for further research and different ways of thinking about human intelligence.

Researcher Mindy L. Kornhaber is an Associate Professor in the Department of Education Policy Studies at The Pennsylvania State University. She holds graduate degrees in Educational Policy and Human Development from Harvard's Graduate School of Education. Kornhaber has suggested that the theory of Multiple Intelligences is so popular within the field of education that it 'validates educators' everyday experience; students think and learn in many ways. It also provides educators with a conceptual framework for organising and reflecting on curriculum assessment and pedagogical practices.

In turn, this reflection has led many educators to develop new approaches that might better meet the needs of the range of learners in their classrooms.

When reading the following information, think about your own child/children and highlight against the following headings as to where you believe their main strengths are, or will be. Then consider how they perform in their current education system.

Visual-Picture Intelligence - is the interpretation and creation of visual images; pictorial imagination and expression; understanding relationship between images and meanings, and between space and effect. The type of roles that hold these talents are artists, designers, cartoonists, story-boarders, architects, photographers, sculptors, town planners, visionaries, inventors, engineers, cosmetics and beauty consultants. Generally, these people learn well from pictures, shapes, images, 3D and use of space.

Linguistic-Verbal Intelligence - is the ability in relation to written and spoken; retention, interpretation and explanation of ideas and information via language, understands relationship between communication and meaning. Such as writers, lawyers, journalists, speakers, trainers, copywriters, English teachers, poets, editors, linguists, translators, PR consultants, media consultants, TV and radio presenters, voice-over artists. These types of people learn well from words and language patterns.

Bodily Kinaesthetic Intelligence - are talented in body movement and control, manual dexterity, physical agility and balance, eye and body co-ordination. These tend to be great as dancers, demonstrators, actors, athletes, divers, sportspeople, soldiers, firefighters, performance artist; ergonomists, osteopaths, fishermen, drivers, craftspeople; gardeners and chefs. They learn well by physical experience and movement, touch and feeling.

Musical Intelligence - is the ability, awareness, and appreciation of sound, recognising tonal and rhythmic patterns, understanding relationships between sound and feelings. The types of people you would expect to have this intelligence are musicians, singers, composers, DJs, music producers, piano tuners, acoustic engineers, entertainers, party planners, environment and noise advisers, voice coaches, and they learn well from rhythm, music and sounds.

Interpersonal Intelligence - easily relating to others are people who are perceptive of other people's feelings; ability to relate to others; interpretation of behaviour and communications; understands the relationships between people and their situations, including other people. Such as therapists, HR professionals, mediators, leaders, counsellors, politicians, educators, salespeople, clergy, psychologists, teachers, doctors, healers, organisers, carers, advertising professionals, coaches and mentors. (There is clear association between this type of intelligence and what is now termed 'Emotional Intelligence' or EQ).

Intrapersonal Intelligence - being great at self-reflection and discovery of themselves is self-awareness, personal cognisance, personal objectivity, the capability to understand oneself, one's relationship to others and the world, and one's own need for, and reaction to change, also closely linked to Emotional Intelligence (EQ). These are generally suited to anyone who is self-aware and involved in the process of changing personal thoughts, beliefs and behaviour in relation to their situation, other people, their purpose and aims, such as counsellors, psychologists, coaches, great leaders able to influence. In this respect there is a similarity to Maslow's Self-Actualisation level, which is a complete fulfilment of self and an understanding of who you are.

Mathematical Intelligence - these people learn well with numbers and logic, detecting patterns, scientific reasoning and deduction; analyse problems, perform mathematical calculations, understands relationship between cause and effect towards a tangible outcome or result, such as scientists, engineers, computer experts, accountants, statisticians, researchers, analysts, traders, bankers, bookmakers, insurance brokers, negotiators, deal-makers, trouble-shooters.

Naturalistic Intelligence - is deemed to be a person's interest in and relationship with the 'natural' world of animals, plants, and the natural work around them. This modality includes people who feel inherently drawn to working in fields that involve animals, plants, geology, along with naturalistic intelligence.

Gardner has discovered more Intelligences since the first 7/8, and the list continues.

The main point to this chapter is that we should be celebrating all the Intelligences, and they should certainly be treated as equally important.

Businesses and organisations thrive on employees that think differently, and by coming together they can achieve amazing things. Afterall, education is about gearing our children up for the 'big world' and if we do not allow them to flourish in the areas of intelligence where they are naturally gifted, many will never flourish and become what they will be great at doing in their lives.

By concentrating on strengths, children will become what they are supposed to become, which in turn will go a long way into making them happy.

Light Bulb Activity

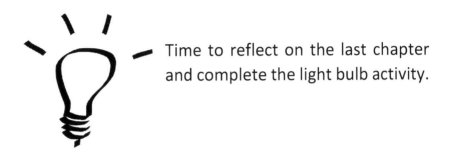

Time to reflect on the last chapter and complete the light bulb activity.

What was interesting in the last chapter?

How can this knowledge be used to your advantage?

Where and when can you implement any new ideas or plans to help with this?

Chapter Seven

Unconscious Bias and Education

"Most teachers waste their time by asking questions which are intended to discover what a pupil does not know, whereas the true art of questioning has for its purpose to discover what the pupil knows or is capable of knowing."

Albert Einstein

So, what is Unconscious Biases? It is stereotyping other people based upon our own opinions stored in the sub and unconscious memory, typically based upon our perception of what is right and wrong, good, bad, or nice.

Generally, we are more comfortable with people who are like us, and sometimes we will feel uncomfortable with somebody or a situation and we don't really know why. It's just a gut feeling.

It's common that we may then consciously or unconsciously change our behaviour towards that person because of this. Whilst this can be either a positive or negative change of course, in some circumstances it could represent an instant dislike or, conversely, an immediate attraction to others.

Sigmund Freud was an Austrian neurologist best known for developing the theories and techniques of psychoanalysis. His research was based on how the mind works in relation to our behaviour, and he categorised the mind into three main levels of consciousness, with the depth of the mind often depicted as an iceberg.

Freud deduced that we use our past influences and experiences to make decisions on a daily basis at a conscious level, much of the decision-making process is actually influenced by our subconscious and unconscious minds, making them 'unconscious decisions'. So, although we make decisions consciously, we do not always make them objectively as they are influenced by so many other factors.

The Conscious Mind contains all the thoughts, memories, feelings and wishes of which we are aware at any given moment. This is the aspect of our mental processing that we can think and talk about in the here and now, although it has limits on the amount of information it can store as we will be cover later in this chapter.

The Sub or Preconscious consists of anything that could potentially be brought into the conscious mind easily when needed.

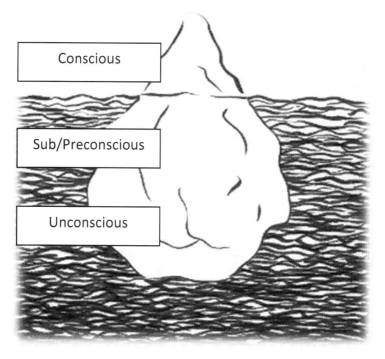

It is a bit like the hard drive of our mind and stores all feelings, emotions, and every experience since our conception.

Amazingly, our Sub or Preconscious can process as many as 20,000 pieces of information at any one time. When hypnosis is used, it is this part of the brain that is accessed and when we make decisions, it is often the influences from this part of the brain that drives the way forward in any given situation.

The Unconscious Mind is a reservoir of feelings, thoughts, urges and memories that are outside of our conscious awareness. However, we are constantly prompted by our unconscious mind which in turn often affects our behaviour and reactions to situations. The Unconscious Mind is where our 'need to survive' and 'fight and flight' systems are triggered.

The interesting part here is that our fight and flight system can be triggered when we are in no danger at all, in fact something as simple as being faced with something or somebody that for whatever reason we do not like. We may even say things like *'I just don't like that person, but I really don't know why.'*

Freud followed the work of Carl Jung, a Swiss psychiatrist and psychoanalyst, who founded analytical psychology. The two thought leaders conducted a lengthy correspondence and collaborated for a while on a joint vision of human psychology.

Often the person who is experiencing the unconscious bias does not realise they are displaying dislike or favouritism and that their behaviours become obvious. Here, many of the signals are created at an unconscious level in the brain and in turn, our behaviour.

The tendency to put certain people in certain boxes based on your own bias, is at an unconscious level. However if you are a learner and you suspect your teacher does not think you are capable of achieving well in their subject, you will quite rightly not be as engaged with anything they try to teach you. This is obviously exceedingly difficult for all involved, however a critical thing to recognise and manage as a teacher is to ensure they get the best out of all learners and control the subliminal behaviour accordingly.

This is incredibly challenging for many, as we constantly transmit our thoughts through our facial expression, body language and voice tonality and do this unconsciously. So, although somebody may try to hide how they feel, often this does not work, and it becomes obvious how the person feels and thinks towards them. Many of our signals are generated from the primal brain (animal brain) in the unconscious memory and we give and receive these signals all the time. Part of this is our need to survive, so the brain makes quick judgements of everybody around us.

So, thinking of this from the moment we are born, we are conditioned with rules, values, and beliefs in relation to what is right and what is wrong. We are constantly influenced with other people's behaviours and belief systems. These are behaviours we adopt and live day by day with and they become who we are. They are what we find to be acceptable and unacceptable behaviours and often are driven by the environments and families we grow up in.

When somebody does not act in the way we believe to be right, we may make snap judgements about them and those around them. We make these decisions, often from ridiculously small amounts of information and within a matter of seconds.

Each of us makes judgements about others, for example, think about a pet peeve (something you dislike) that others do, such as someone not saying 'thank you' when you hold a door open for them and they walk through without any acknowledgement nor gesture of appreciation.

Think about how you react when somebody acts in the way you dislike or do not approve of.

Even if you don't show your distaste, you will probably still have a very strong opinion about it. You may even share this with others around you or when you get home tell your partner or family about what happened, as it sticks with you as not right.

The offensive behaviour of somebody else is often completely unintentional, however we translate that behaviour and, very cleverly, our brain makes up stories such as that person was being disrespectful or discourteous.

We may also have opinions ingrained into our thought processes about other people based upon where they live, how they speak and how they behave in general. As we mature, we may challenge our thoughts and opinions based on new experiences we encounter. Sometimes we realise that our thoughts and feelings towards a person or situation is unfounded and we then recondition our thoughts to think differently.

At an unconscious level, we are constantly triggered with information that makes us respond to situations. Some of these triggers are known as unconditional reflexes which may manifest in us blinking or sneezing. However, we also have our conditioned reflex, which is a learned reflex in a situation where we see danger or something that we perceive to be a threat.

In some situations, for example the workplace, we may expect others to look a certain way, talk a certain way, think a certain way, smell a certain way, and act a certain way. When they do not, we notice they are different to us, and we make judgements about them within a split second. We may even think that their behaviour is so different that we cannot tolerate them.

This is one of the fantastic things about the human brain; imagination. Based upon our rules, values, and beliefs about life, we instantaneously judge situations, and our imagination will run away with all sorts of stories convincing us that we are right.

This is often referred to as the 'Stimulus and Response'. In other words, something stimulates us, and we immediately react to the situation.

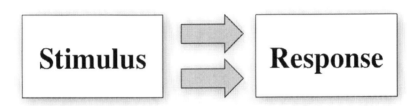

This reaction is so immediate that we do not have time to engage any rational thinking behind what has occurred. And sometimes, our fight and flight system is automatically engaged so we may start to feel the effects of adrenaline running around our body, making the heart pump faster and creating anxieties towards a person or situation.

This is the system we were born with and it is there to protect us from danger. However, the failing of this innate system is that it is often triggered, enabling us to be stronger and think more quickly, when in reality, we are in no danger at all. As a result, we are left with the effects of heightened adrenaline pumping around the body with no use for it. Although this is completely natural, the effects can be longer lasting.

Often in these situations we find it difficult to keep our responses hidden and our emotions and reactions become transparent, for example, our faces, body posture and voice may change, so our thoughts become obvious.

We make judgements about them within split seconds. It is easy to understand why we react in this way. All the rules, the do's and the don'ts, that we learn when we are incredibly young, along with the culture that has shown us what is normal and correct are 'recorded' in our memories. Additionally, we usually store decisions made at important time in our lives.

We have endless messages from all the mediums in society such as television, magazines, and newspapers, along with influences from friends, family, and the opinions they have of others.

Our experiences may also influence what we feel, think, and do. For example, somebody may decide not to travel on a train after a bad experience, or a person who once had financial problems might decide never to waste money. We call this kind of rule a 'personal record'. It plays repeatedly, repeating old messages, telling us what to do and how to act.

When we act in accordance with our personal records, we generally feel comfortable and secure. When others act in accordance with our records, we feel comfortable and secure around them. However, when somebody does not behave in the way we expect, we can become uneasy and it may even trigger our dislike for the person.

The basic facts are everybody is unique and, importantly, so too are our children. Our maps of our worlds run deep and our view of right and wrong can be extremely vast, so when we bring many people into one environment to learn, there are many complications that must be considered.

Firstly, all the learners will have different upbringings and experiences, a barometer or moral compass of what they consider to be is right and wrong. Accordingly, this in turn will influence and determine how they behave and conduct themselves. The difficulty with this is that all teaching cultures should consider how they will set the right parameters to ensure that people know how to behave within their environments, however this is far easier said than done.

Secondly, the need to teach 'non-biased' behaviours is critical if we want to have healthy learning environments. Leading by example in acceptance of other's opinions and values and celebrating them. So, teaching this in schools is vital if we want to work towards a tolerant world.

We all have 'unconscious biases' built on our own upbringings and it is vitally important that we lead by example and do not show we have favourites or preferences when we teach our learners. The impact of favouritism can be completely damaging and make learners feel or think that they are being treated differently. Naturally, this will result in negative behaviours from those individuals.

The additional challenge for teachers is that some children and parents will also have an 'unconscious bias' towards them, which again can be negative.

This is because our brain makes snap judgements based on our immediate thoughts and this is also influenced from our need to survive. Our brain picks up every action of another person and will often make its mind up before we are consciously aware as to whether the person is going to be good for us or not.

Like most parents, we all have ideas and aspirations for our children, driven by our love for them to be safe, happy, and successful. We know that education plays a large part in giving our children options that will hopefully ensure they go on to live fulfilled lives.

When you first had your child, you would of course have aspirations for them and naturally we attempt to influence what our children do, based on our own opinions and conditioning.

We already know that the need to write, spell and understand the fundamentals of mental arithmetic is important. However, we also know that many pupils will not become the next leading scientists, doctors or lawyers, and actually they may never want to be either.

Our criteria for benchmarking is often not conducive to how so many individuals' brains work and that we are educating based on a set of criteria that has been introduced by governing bodies, who in my opinion maybe detached from the main needs of societies in many instances. Despite this, our children are forced to follow that set curriculum regardless of what importance or priority they may place on any given subject in relation to their own aspirations.

Although it makes sense to follow a national curriculum, it must be questioned how well-researched it is to meet the demands of modern life. We need to establish *'what are we educating our young to become?'* and *'how are we measuring their success, other than grades and results?'*

For some, academic achievement is absolutely the right route, but it is also worth considering that for other children, their raw talent will not be in academia, as their skills and talents lie in other areas.

And for those children who have talents in different topics, we need to ask a simple question: does achieving highly in academia mean that the child grows into a happy adult with skills and capabilities for the outside world and the careers they may choose?

We all too often have opinions and unconscious bias of our own children and indeed, other people's children, which may not always be well founded and accurate in relation to intelligence, raw talent and abilities. These opinions can often be negative and are a distorted view from a select few who govern the criteria to determine whether a young person is likely to be seen as successful in life. And as we know, our view will be due to our conditioning in life.

The opinions of other parents, teachers, family. and friends is too freely shared based upon academia as to whether a child is clever or not talented.

So, how do we measure intelligence? We are conditioned to believe that intelligent people are those who pass all their exams with flying colours and attain impressive academic qualifications as a result. This enables them to go to university, achieve their dreams and build happy and successful careers. Obviously for those people who aspire to do this, that is a perfect destination.

Because of our conditioning we may have an unconscious bias to believe others who do not achieve this same level of academic accomplishment through university are not as bright or clever. However today, there are many routes to building a successful career, such as apprenticeship schemes. Although these schemes were originally more limited, they have been created with businesses to build careers for many talented individuals, such as solicitors, plumbers, aerospace engineers, software developers, marine pilots, accountants and so on. This means that your child can get on-the-job experience, whilst being free of university course fees and accruing huge debt from student loans.

So, it is wise to recognise that we have been conditioned with 'unconscious bias' that causes great anxiety for many parents and children feeling that they need to achieve the best possible academic results and qualifications in order to have happy and successful children. However, it is wise to consider that there are many other options and routes to success in life. Our goal as parents is to develop our young into being happy, well-adjusted individuals with the ability to contribute their talents to society. Unfortunately, we are too often doing the opposite and are developing adults with limiting beliefs and low self-esteem which will run deep with them for life.

As already suggested, this of course is often completely unintentional and yet can have such a deep effect.

The effect may be that the child is left feeling they have completely failed, not just in education, but even worse, failed their parents, guardians or carers, and this generally will manifest itself into a long-lasting emotional feeling of inadequacy.

Thinking about the need to belong and our need to feel safe and attached to something or someone, this can be extremely negative for a child's self-esteem.

And of course, it is worth being mindful of the fact that some great success stories come from failure and when someone thinks they will never be able to achieve something and keep getting something wrong, they still learn. In time and with the right support, they will finally achieve their goal, learning that perseverance is the route to success. However, we must also be mindful that we all need different things in our journey of learning and one thing for certain is we need to be flexible and adaptive.

In order for someone to develop and grow, they need to get used to making mistakes and not being successful at everything they do, so in turn, we must not punish failure and instead recognise it as part of life's rich tapestry.

If we just teach in one method in one way, we are pre-empting failure by not providing the right framework for support to help everybody succeed.

Understandably, we of course all want children to become independent, self-sufficient and above all happy, and for that reason we need to challenge whether the emotional damage we can inflict is worth it in the long run.

By conditioning ourselves to think differently about education and opening our minds to elevating all subjects, we may find we have a world of happier and contented children, learning skills and growing into careers that they actually enjoy and be proud of. We also may find that by teaching subjects such as psychology and Unconscious Bias from an early age, we will empower our children to firstly understand themselves, and in turn understand those around them. Teaching Emotional Intelligence of self-awareness, self-management, social awareness, and social management is a way to reduce Unconscious Bias and create acceptance of everybody, everywhere.

Activity

If you would like to try an activity, think of yourself and what you consider to be your values, beliefs, and rules and what you expect from others in return.

Then consider the world through somebody else's eyes and decide whether you can exercise more tolerance in situations that you do not see eye-to-eye on.

Then, answer the following questions:

What behaviours would you consider to be common courtesy? For example, when someone says please or thank you.

What do you think about someone who does not use the same common courtesies that are important to you?

How do you let them know you do not approve?

Based on the Unconscious Bias chapter, how can you adapt your reactions in those situations?

Light Bulb Activity

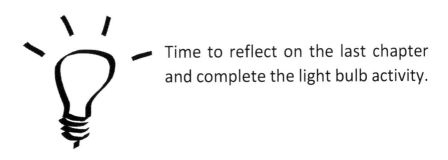

Time to reflect on the last chapter and complete the light bulb activity.

What was interesting in the last chapter?

How can this knowledge be used to your advantage?

Where and when can you implement any new ideas or plans to help with this?

Chapter Eight

Communication, the Brain and Learning

"When someone helping you gets frustrated, don't let them. Take a step back, because you can't learn anything under pressure. And don't worry about the label!"

Erin Brockovich

As we already know, the moment a child is born they are listening, watching, touching, tasting, and smelling everything around them to help them learn about the environment they are in. We shape who they will become as an adult right from the word go. A child listens to how their family speak to each other, the tone of the voice and the words that they use, observing body postures and facial expressions that are being displayed, often completely unconsciously by the adult.

Our memory is a group of systems that work together to enable the storage of information. The more relevant and enjoyable the experience of learning something, the more likely we are to store the information for a longer period.

Information enters the brain through our senses and this first stage of our memory is often referred to as the 'sensory memory'. Information will only be recalled for a second or so and this will depend upon how important that the learner determines the information to be and use. If it is seen to be important, it will enter the 'short-term memory' which is part of the 'working memory'.

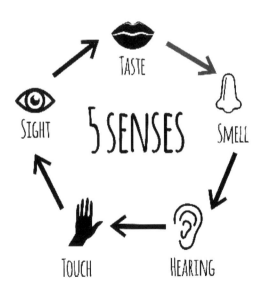

The 'short-term memory' will store this information for around 15 to 30 seconds and it is important at this point that the information is embedded, either through repetition, or through experiencing what is happening, which helps our brain to get the information to stick. It is particularly important when we teach to contextualise the information so that the learner can see where the information fits into the 'big picture' or slots into the 'jigsaw' of life, creating building blocks of information which build a pattern or create a picture that make the information interesting for the brain.

As we are all so different, this is often where the challenges begin in the learning journey for any teacher. What one person perceives to be important or interesting, another may not. What one person likes to do to learn, another may find difficult. If we do not manage to store the information in the 'short-term memory' it will then be lost.

Three-Stage Process of Memory

Information enters through the Sensory System where it is retained for second or so. Selective Attention then moves the information into Short-Term Memory where it is held while attention (Rehearsal) continues. If the information receives enough Rehearsal, it will then enter and be stored in the Long-Term Memory for a time.

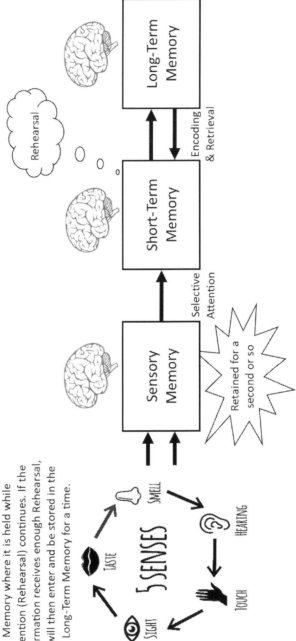

The important thing about this is that if the learner only picks up part of the information or pattern, the memory may not be correct and recall accurately the right information. This means that we will naturally make mistakes, which is why checking that the learner has correctly stored the right information is important.

The facts are that two peoples' account of any experience will often be vastly different, which is why recapping, providing time for discussions and reflection and checking learning is vitally important.

The 'short-term memory' is also restricted in the amount of information it can retain, which was evidenced by George Miller's study of the 'short-term memory'. Here. Miller discovered that this part of our memory can only remember between five to nine pieces of information at any one time. The study, known as the *'Magic Number Seven'* found that in order to retain information, we need to 'chunk' it together into sets of three. For example, telephone numbers are often recalled in three chunks, as follows: 012345678 would be recalled as 012-345-678.

So, to recap:

- Our sensory memory forgets within a second or so.
- We contextualise information in hugely different ways, which means that we all remember different pieces of information.

- Our brain easily gets overloaded with too much information.
- Information may be inaccurately recalled, as we only remember parts of the message.
- When overloaded our 'short-term memory' will often delete what it believes to be unimportant.
- Recall and repetition is vitally important to embed information into our long-term memory.
- Testing and checking that the information is correct is critical.

Once we have retained the information in our 'short-term memory' we are then able to store it in our 'long-term memory'. Having said this, over time our memory will begin to forget some of the information if it is not used. If, however, we initially learnt through physical learning (touch, taste and smell also referred to as *'Kinaesthetic'*) and combine this with sight and sound, we are more likely to retain it as this plays back as an experience, rather than is stored in our long-term memory. If we rely solely on sight and sound repeating like flash cards, we are more likely to forget this quickly if not used given that the brain will not retain it as effectively.

So, understanding that learning through our senses will first enter our 'sensory memory', another interesting fact was proven by Professor Ruth Fridman in her 2000 study which proved that children can hear when in the womb.

It was found that babies' heart rates increased and that they moved around in rhythm to the music. Once born, the children responded more to certain types of music and if the children had been played certain songs before they were born, by nine months old they were able to imitate the same piece of music.

Like most parents you compare your child to other children of a similar age to see how they are developing and making sure that they are 'on track'. This is very normal for all of us, as we want our child to have the best life possible and we measure this by comparisons.

The basic facts are the only way we give and receive information is through our five senses. This is clear when we watch a baby learning.

Firstly, we know they grab for objects and then put just about everything straight into their mouth, make gurgling noises, respond to being comforted, enjoy their milk and as they grow into toddlers, often refuse to eat certain food. We then encourage different flavours, some they like, others they do not. We, as our babies, infants, children, and teens, are all naturally different.

As a child develops, we may discourage our children from touching certain objects or putting them straight into their mouth, however we know that this is how a baby learns so quickly and in fact, more than at any other time in their lives.

The development of a child's brain is tremendous from birth until three years of age. At birth, a baby's brain has all the neurons it will ever have and by the first year of life, it will have doubled in size. By the age of three, a child's brain will be 80% of its adult size. It is constantly building over a million neuron connections every second, which means the importance of relationships, experiences and their environment have huge influences which are crucial to the brain's development.

There are many factors that affect how well the brain develops. In addition to genetics such as nutrition, experiences with others and whether they have been exposed to infections or toxins, along with healthy nurturing and care, are paramount for a child's development.

Children learn constantly to build their brain capacity by using all their senses of touch, taste, smell, sight, and hearing and this does not change with age.

When we then start to restrict the tools we use to learn, such as removing the touch and feeling aspect of learning, the brain will automatically crave this to help the learning process. This is when we may become fidgety and restless, as the brain feels it is being starved of something it believes it needs to get the full picture.

Eventually the brain will become uninterested and switch off completely, meaning it has become bored, or even impatient waiting for the right stimulus. This is often when people may experience either lethargy or heavy eyes during a lesson. Unfortunately, the behaviour patterns in some learners may then become rebellious and even disruptive.

It is obvious that we want our children to be safe, so we may take something dangerous away from them. To keep a child safe is obviously very important, however the power of taste and smell combined is so critical for their development, and this same fundamental need or requirement doesn't change when they are learning at school.

If therefore, we cannot always provide a physical aspect to a lesson, we must always provide context and where the subject matter fits into their life. In other words, where is it relevant to them and why are they learning it.

This helps the child to understand the emotional aspects of the subject, which are strongly linked to feelings we gain from touch, taste, and smell (Kinaesthetic). We, in a way, need to regenerate the stimulus of these senses. If we fail to do this and concentrate on hearing and seeing completely, the learning will become much harder for the brain to absorb and it may get very bored.

During the early years, we are constantly teaching our children how to behave, whether this is a deliberate act, or an observation of our own behaviour that they are mirroring.

We take our children to playgroups and activities to help them learn how to interact and behave, how to share and play with others. They do this kinaesthetically with activities and toys, singing rhymes and songs and gaining the overall experiences of everything around them. Although we do try and teach them to sit and listen, they generally cannot do this without becoming extremely bored, as children need stimulation on all levels in order to help them develop and grow.

By the time our children start nursery they have learnt certain behaviours which give them their identity and personalities. This is when the education system kicks in.

All brains love to be inspired and the more the whole brain is stimulated, the faster we learn and, importantly, retain what we have learnt.

Have you ever wondered why slime and squidges, fidget spinners and scented pens are so popular amongst children? I recently introduced fidget spinners into my training room of adults and was surprised to see just how many of my learners were using them along with other training toys that stimulate and accelerate their learning. These tools, without a doubt, help maintain the attention span of grown-ups, so why would they not do the same for children in mainstream schools. After all, most of us like to fidget with something, it helps our propensity to remember things.

We have all probably experienced being on a phone call or in a meeting and started scribbling or doodling on a pad, drawing pictures or patterns, or making countless notes that you will never read in detail again.

Our brain triggers this when it gets bored, it starts craving physical stimulation. The more we stimulate all our senses, the more we learn. And the more we create an experience of that learning, the more likely we are to retain the information.

The theory of the brain having two hemispheres is well-researched; that the left brain controls logic and detail and the right brain controls big picture, emotion, and creativity. This means that the world is observed differently.

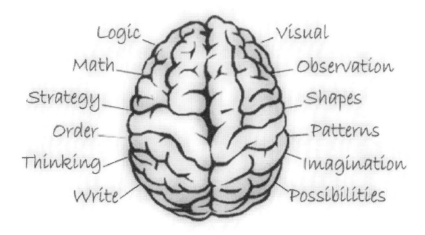

It follows that any learning intervention will always be more beneficial if both sides of the brain are stimulated and working together.

When we teach, if we educate concentrating on just one side of the brain, many learners will get bored very quickly and generally do not learn as well.

In addition, most people have a tendency to be dominant in either the left brain or right brain, so if you have a classroom of 31 learners and only teach left brain activities, all the right brain dominated learners will become bored pretty quickly, and potentially become disengaged.

The challenges are that once we restrict the brain and enter into a desk-based classroom situation, unless we vary the methods of teaching and create sensory stimulation, our communication is stripped back to a level where many brains will struggle to concentrate for long periods of time. The learning then becomes harder, and for many, this becomes difficult. The brain will naturally start wandering and thinking of things it enjoys doing.

Interestingly, studies have proven that children diagnosed as having ADHD or Dyslexia tend to be more dominant in the right hemisphere of the brain. Yet, although there is much research to support these findings, this doesn't seem to be taken into consideration in the way we teach in schools to support right brain dominated children.

There are many advantages of being dominant in the right hemisphere of the brain. Such children, and indeed adults, are said to be much more holistic, intuitive, and empathetic. They tend to have an emotional outlook on the world, one with wide-focus, flexibility, creativity, and a humorous approach to life. By contrast, the left brain is based very much on focussing on detail, organisation, logic, and control which all lend well to the academic Intelligences, particularly in mathematics, English, and sciences.

Interestingly, research by Dr Sherman of Harvard Busines School in the United States found that the dyslexic brain may be bigger than the ordinary brain, highlighting three main biological differences. Although dyslexia can affect people in varying ways, the most common difficulty is with memory and languages. For example, mechanics that have dyslexia have been known to look at an engine and quickly understand how everything is connected and are easily able to see the best solution to a practical problem. They are also generally extremely practical in their thinking, and although people who have dyslexia face particular challenges, they have great advantages in relation to physical co-ordination skills. They are also often artistically gifted.

In fact, often a dyslexic learner's greatest barrier to becoming successful can be a lack of confidence and low self-esteem due to them feeling they are not as gifted as others. Devastatingly for them, due to their preferred way of learning, they are too frequently made to feel they are not bright. This creates limiting beliefs and can leave them thinking or feeling inferior or worthless.

Some very well-known dyslexic people that have been extremely successful are:

Steve Jobs, Richard Branson, John Lennon, George Washington, Albert Einstein, Walt Disney, Winston Churchill, and Tommy Hilfiger.

The list goes on and on...

In relation to ADHD, there really hasn't been enough research into the actual experience of being ADHD. However, studies by Professor Iain D Gilchrist explains that the right brain is more neurologically 'tightly connected' than the left, signalling travel shorter distances with less chance of signal decay. More importantly the right brain uses noradrenaline (norepinephrine), rather than dopamine for communications.

Research shows dopamine as the 'weakness' with the neurotransmitter prevalent in people with ADHD, so logically you might expect the left brain to be affected, not the right? Many extremely successful people who have been diagnosed with ADHD are:

Olympian Simone Biles, Henry Ford, Beethoven, Ryan Gosling, Ed Hallowell, Ernest Hemingway, Woodrow Wilson, Tom Cruise, Pablo Picasso, F W Woolworth, Thomas Edison and Albert Einstein.

And in fact, many have both diagnosis such as: Albert Einstein, Winston Churchill, Walt Disney, Robin Williams, Richard Branson amongst hundreds, if not thousands, of others. However, if their successes were dependent upon academic attainment alone, they may have been left behind.

By fighting off the stigma and negative branding associated with these conditions in school, the aforementioned people not only became incredibly successful, but in fact, became famed for their successes. Sadly, others may fall by the wayside and struggle with levels of low self-esteem and inferiority complexes throughout their lives.

I will cover more on this later in the book, however this means that when we design any learning initiative, we must consider how we are communicating the subject through all the senses and what the brain needs to enjoy the learning experience, which in turn means information is more likely to be retained within the long-term memory.

Thereafter, we stimulate both hemispheres of the brain by providing logic and facts, along with the experiences and emotional aspects, required to make the information memorable. An example of this would be when we introduce learning practices into Maths, such as role-playing a shop keeper, or business meeting discussing the profit and loss accounts, or financial negotiations. The whole roleplay makes the learning an experiential and therefore more memorable for all learners. Some of course will enjoy watching or observing, others will enjoy the detail of facts, whilst others will enjoy acting the parts of the role-play. And although this is only one example, all learning can be made enjoyable for all.

Other examples could be learning the solar system by physically assembling it to scale by using modelling to provide the experience of building the planets and where they are placed in the galaxy, again creates an experience for the learner. This, backed up with logical facts and information and mathematics for scaling, makes the whole experience enjoyable and, more importantly, memorable.

In Biology, learning about the skeleton, students could be asked to build models to scale and label them. This is important at any age, from birth to adult life in any learning experience.

Obviously for some subjects, this is much easier than others, however it takes a lot of planning to ensure that lessons are stimulating for all learners and often something that is difficult when facing the challenges of the antiquated system we find our children in.

One way to think about this is if you have attended a presentation or speech where you are sitting for a long period, probably over 10 to 15 minutes, often the brain will go to sleep. Some people may experience heavy eyes or feel the need to fidget. This is very natural and is a sign that the brain is craving more stimulation to stay focused.

The difficultly in teaching is always how to keep your audience interested and engaged, in fact, motivated to learn what you are teaching. This is even more important if the subject matter is particularly dry or difficult to grasp.

Now think about sitting at a desk for several hours at a time, whilst somebody talks to you and fires questions to the group in anticipation of getting an answer. Without a doubt, some learners will be able to respond much more quickly than others and this may depend on their own preferred way of learning.

But now, put yourself in the position of a learner who is particularly analytical or reflective. That person may want longer to assess whether that information is accurate and correct, whereas a more naturally outgoing character may be happy to answer and not worry so much as to whether the answer is correct or not.

Again, we are all absolutely unique in our learning and communication, which often is completely misunderstood and hence creates a negative learning experience for many children.

So, what happens to the children who do not react or respond quickly, or the child who becomes disengaged? Of course, this is the challenge for many teachers, particularly when class sizes are so large. As all brains learn in unique ways, learning material should be adapted to suit all pupils, rather than using one method of delivery and expecting that to suit the whole class's learning styles.

Light Bulb Activity

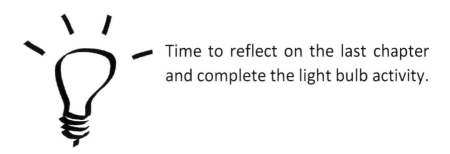 Time to reflect on the last chapter and complete the light bulb activity.

What was interesting in the last chapter?

How can this knowledge be used to your advantage?

Where and when can you implement any new ideas or plans to help with this?

Chapter Nine

Adapting to Stimulate Learning

"Imagination is more important than knowledge. For knowledge is limited to all we now know and understand, while imagination embraces the entire world, and all there ever will be to know and understand."

Albert Einstein

In addition to how we receive, use and store information there has been much research into how we learn and there are two well-known models.

Kolb's Model and Honey and Mumford's variation of the Kolb's Model.

Peter Honey and Alan Mumford developed their learning styles variation on the Kolb model while working on a project together for the Chloride Corporation in the 1970's.

Honey and Mumford were quoted in relation to their model as follows:

"Our description of the stages in the learning cycle originated from the work of David Kolb. Kolb uses different words to describe the stages of the learning cycle and four learning styles, however the similarities between his model and ours are greater than the differences."

Peter Honey

Although Honey and Mumford acknowledge that their Learning Styles Model was based on Kolb's work, it is different, and they label their four styles as:

- Activist
- Reflector
- Theorist
- Pragmatist

Activist – 'Having an Experience' and being in the 'here and now', gregarious, seek challenge and immediate experience, open-minded, bored with implementation.

Activists involve themselves fully and without bias in new experiences. They enjoy the here and now and are happy to be dominated by immediate experiences. They are open-minded and not sceptical, and this tends to make them enthusiastic about anything new. They will try anything once. Tending to act first and consider the consequences afterwards so their days are filled with activity. They enjoy tackling problems, however as soon as the excitement from one activity has died down, they are busy looking for the next one. Thriving on new experiences and challenges, they tend to get bored with implementation and longer-term consolidation. They are gregarious people constantly involving themselves with others but, in doing so; they seek to centre all activities around themselves.

Reflectors – 'Reviewing the Experience', 'standing back', gathering data, pondering and analysing, delay reaching conclusions, listen before speaking, thoughtful.

Reflectors like to stand back to ponder experiences and observe them from many different perspectives. They collect data, both first-hand and from others, and prefer to think about it thoroughly before coming to any conclusion. The thorough collection and analysis of data about experiences and events is what counts so they tend to postpone reaching definitive conclusions for as long as possible. Their philosophy is to be cautious. They are thoughtful people who like to consider all possible angles and implications before making a move. They prefer to take a back seat in meetings and discussions. They enjoy observing other people in action. They listen to others and get the drift of the discussion before making their own points. They tend to adopt a low profile and have a slightly distant, tolerant unruffled air about them. When they act it is part of a wide picture, which includes the past as well as the present and others' observations as well as their own.

Theorist – 'Concluding from the Experience', thinking things through in logical steps, assimilate disparate facts into coherent theories, rationally objective, reject subjectivity and flippancy.

Theorists adapt and integrate observations into complex but logically sound theories. They think problems through in a vertical step-by-step logical way. They assimilate disparate facts into coherent theories. They tend to be perfectionists who won't rest easy until things are tidy and fit into a rational scheme. They like to analyse and synthesise. They are keen on basic assumptions, principles, theories, models, and systems thinking. Their philosophy prizes rationality and logic. *'If it's logical, it's good.'* Questions they frequently ask are: *'Does it make sense?'*; *'How does this fit with that?'*; *'What are the basic assumptions?'* They tend to be detached, analytical and dedicated to rational objectivity.

Pragmatists – 'Planning the next steps', seeking and trying out new ideas, practical, down-to-earth, enjoy problem solving and decision-making quickly, bored with long discussions.

Subjective or ambiguous. Their approach to problems is consistently logical. This is their 'mental set' and they rigidly reject anything that doesn't fit with it. They prefer to maximise certainty and feel uncomfortable with subjective judgements, lateral thinking, and anything flippant.

Pragmatists are keen on trying out ideas, theories, and techniques to see if they work in practice. They positively search out new ideas and take the first opportunity to experiment with applications. They are the sort of people who return from management courses brimming with new ideas that they want to try out in practice. They like to get on with things and act quickly and confidently on ideas that attract them. They tend to be impatient with ruminating and open-ended discussions. They are essentially practical, down-to-earth people who like making practical decisions and solving problems. They respond to problems and opportunities as a challenge. Their philosophy is 'there is always a better way' and 'if it works, its good.'

There is a strong argument to link the Honey and Mumford stages to the Kolb learning styles as follows and in the diagram.

Activist	-	Accommodating
Reflector	-	Diverging
Theorist	-	Assimilating
Pragmatist	-	Converging

The following diagram reflects the previous point.

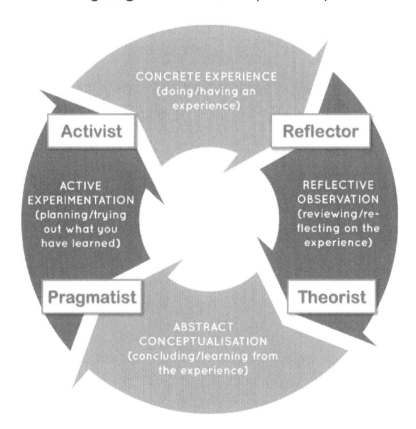

If our learners do not get stimulated in all the ways in which they learn, then learning will not be as effective. All learning should be designed with elements for each style of learning to stimulate the brain. If we fail to do this, the brain will get bored and switch off.

Learning Activity

If you wish to understand your child's preferred learning style, ask them to complete the following tables. Once completed, discuss examples of each.

Ask their teacher if you can sit in one of their lessons to observe how the lessons suits your child's style.

When completing this activity, there are no right or wrong answers.

Activist	Like	Dislike
Being asked to complete an exercise without knowledge		
Getting engrossed in quick activities with no planning		
High energy, excitement, and drama		
Taking the lead and being the centre of attention		
When things suddenly change with no prior warning		
I often talk before thinking		
Total		

Reflectors	Like	Dislike
Watching others in class		
Seeing how things develop before I join in		
Thinking before acting		
To decide what to say before I speak		
I prefer a quiet approach		
Enjoy seeing others discuss topics and learn well from that		
Total		

Theorists	Like	Dislike
Facts of situation before acting		
Working on my own		
Details of a topic before I act		
Knowing information about a topic before speaking about it		
I am not overly emotional in school		
I only act when I have all the information		
Total		

Pragmatists	Like	Dislike
Putting facts and theories into practice		
Discussing topics with others		
Practical activities backed up with facts		
The opportunity to ask questions as I am learning		
Try new stuff out once I have some information		
Group activities in a classroom		
Total		

What were your scores?

	Like	Dislike
Activist		
Reflector		
Theorist		
Pragmatist		

You may find that you fit into all the boxes, however we tend to be dominant in one or two areas of the model and although we can learn in all four ways, we generally have strong preferences.

When a teacher designs any learning intervention, it should follow the four main ways in which we like to learn. That way, we get balance and generally more engagement from everybody. It is about making the learning relevant and enjoyable at the same time. Our brain can then contextualise it and therefore more likely to remember it.

If we just rely on repetition, then the information will not be as deeply embedded into the unconscious mind and becomes easier to forget.

Light Bulb Activity

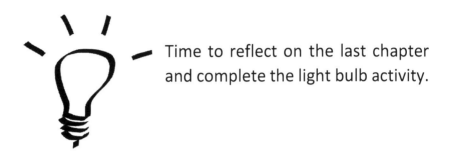

Time to reflect on the last chapter and complete the light bulb activity.

What was interesting in the last chapter?

How can this knowledge be used to your advantage?

Where and when can you implement any new ideas or plans to help with this?

Chapter Ten

Having Fun While Learning

"We stigmatise mistakes. And we're now running national educational systems where mistakes are the worst thing you can make -- and the result is that we are educating people out of their creative capacities."

Sir Ken Robinson

Children are born knowing that learning is fun, and this has no parameters regardless of gender, origin, race, disability, or religion. Babies giggle when they see a happy face, they constantly look for interaction. Like everybody, they are born knowing that comfort, love, and acceptance is enjoyable and innately there is a strong need to feel safe and cared about.

The facts are that communication and how we learn is in no doubt a very complex subject and although this may seem obvious, it is important to recognise that all messages from one person's brain to another are sent and received via our senses, as previously discussed in this book.

If we put this in the context of a very young child learning, they use touch, taste, smell, sight and hearing to learn from the moment they are born. This learning through senses does not change with age.

Continuously using five senses they receive and provide information. When your child was born, I would imagine, like most parents, you spent hours watching them learn and interact with you, the family and in fact anybody they could gain attention from. Why? Because this is how all of us learn and continue to learn throughout our whole lives.

You are probably familiar with the 'soft spot' on a baby's head. The soft spot is formally referred to as the **fontanelles**, and is there until the skull is fully fused together between the ages of 9 to 18 months. As we know, this is to help the head fit through the birth canal, however it is also to ensure that the brain can grow quickly during early childhood. When they reach around three years old, your child's brain will be about 80% the size of an adult brain.

Early in your child's life, they will start to form synapses which are the junctions between two nerve cells, consisting of a minute gap across which impulses pass by diffusion of a neurotransmitter. This happens at a faster rate than any other time in their life and many more than needed are created, enabling them to learn more quickly than an adult.

All children are unique and have their own traits, however the brain development is heavily influenced by external elements or factors.

We know that the genes (nature) feed this mass synapse formation, however the environment (nurture) helps the brain decide which pathways to keep and which ones to erase.

The more often a synapse is used, or the more often a skill or idea is practiced or heard, the stronger that synapse gets. This means that things that are used often, like language and walking, stay ingrained in a child's brain, while things that are neglected disappear. This process also happens in adults' brains, but at a much slower rate.

Because your baby is rapidly creating and pruning out synapses, this is a critical period for learning things. It also means that without practice, certain skills will disappear.

If you want to create lasting skills in your child (like a second language) it is imperative that their exposure and practice is constant. Children's 'flexible' brains provide a unique opportunity to create a solid foundation on which to build for the rest of their lives.

Our brains need to be stimulated to grow and to do this all parts of the brain should be stimulated. We should be using both the right and left side of the brain, left for logic, mathematical and linguistic abilities, and the right for creativity, emotion, and ideas. In fact, we know these are critical in our daily activities, yet in our education system there is a strong expectation that our children can concentrate for long periods using the left hemisphere and little stimulation of the right. By having little expression in exercises, thoughts and feelings and concentrating mainly on exercising only the left hemisphere, for logic, facts and figures, it's is no wonder children become bored.

Our education system concentrates on mainly two ways to give and receive information; auditory and visual. It has to be said that during the observations of seeing my own children develop, some teachers introduce varying methods to maintain interest such as music, rhymes, treats and water breaks. Given that we know this stimulates the senses, this will help with fun element of learning and moreover, retention of the information learnt. Unfortunately, these techniques are not standard practice in so many schools, so is entirely depended on the teacher's individual style and delivery.

As discussed, children generally love squidges, slime, putty, and fidget spinners. Similarly, most children enjoy making things with paper mâché, painting, drawing, sewing, woodwork, metalwork, discussing subjects, group quizzes, outdoor activities, sport, music, the list goes on. However, these activities are not introduced freely into lessons, in fact in many schools, it's quite the opposite.

We expect children of all ages to sit, look and listen for long periods of time with no fidgeting or interruptions. If adults were subjected to the same conditions, very few would be able to concentrate either.

In business meetings, or while you are on a call, you will naturally find yourself doodling on a pad or fidgeting with an object. This is purely because the brains need to stay awake and stay stimulated. Think of how many people in such an environment hold a pen, even if they're not writing anything down. This is not a disorder, but rather an innate need to stay engaged at an unconscious level.

How many adults do you know that can sit and watch a presentation for more than 10 minutes without being bored, unless different mediums of delivery are being used such as interactive question and answer sessions, activities or video clips with humour.

As a professional communication trainer, I personally have been delivering courses to groups for over 25 years and presenting for even longer. It is normal for an audience to become restless if the presentation bores them, so what is the difference between teaching adults and teaching children? Absolutely nothing! By stimulating all the senses and all Intelligences, we avoid the brain becoming bored. Bored children are no different to bored adults. Both become disengaged, possibly disruptive and at times, rebellious all due to the lack of stimulation in learning. The difference is, adults generally have choices as to where they decide to work, however children, unfortunately, do not.

An example of where we can challenge the way in which we teach linguistics and literacy skills is outlined in the work by Professor Stephen Krashen, who is a leading world scholar of Education at the University of Southern California, and author of several books on language acquisition.

In a publication on 9th January 2006, Krashen cites the following:

'Instead of making learning to read a pleasure by embracing Sustained Silent Reading (SSR), we've made it a pain by subjecting youngsters to massive doses of phonics instruction. But the real challenge of transforming today's

children into competent readers isn't about teaching them the basics (sooner or later, nearly all children get them). It's about helping students develop richer vocabularies, understand complex oral and written language, and become proficient writers and reasonably accurate spellers. In other words, it's about moving children to higher levels of literacy. The agony and the evidence over the past 20 years, I've reviewed scores of studies that have compared students in classes that include SSR with those that don't, and I'm confident that children who read for pleasure do as well or better than their SSR-deprived peers. And the longer the programme, the greater the gains. In eight out of ten studies that tracked pupils in long-term SSR programmes of 12 months or more, students who read recreationally outperformed their counterparts in classes that lacked leisure reading—and in the other two studies, there was no difference between the two groups.

Research has also shown that SSR is at least as effective as conventional teaching methods in helping children acquire those aspects of reading that are measured by standardised tests, and pleasure reading provides a great deal that these tests don't measure. Study after study has confirmed that those who read more know more about a wide variety of topics. Plus, according to both students and teachers, SSR is a much more pleasant approach than regular skill-building instruction. The most negative research result one comes across is that some SSR and comparison groups make the same gains. For the most part, studies that show no difference between the two groups are short-term, some lasting as little as eight to ten weeks. Many short-term SSR programmes are effective, but there's a good reason these programmes aren't even more successful. It takes readers time to find a book that's right for them and that leaves students with less time for reading. When we give readers more time, the results strongly favour SSR.'

In other words, less traditional instruction may be a good thing for children by allowing them to read anything they find interesting, whether this is comics, magazines, book from the shelf or even on a kindle.

Providing we give children time and access to reading books they enjoy and take an interest in, they will gain most of the phonics and literacy skills they need for life. And importantly, they will enjoy reading, which is most of the battle with getting children to read in the first place.

In addition, constant testing often has an adverse effect to children feeling motivated to read and write as they do not see it as a pleasant pastime, they start to view it as a constant challenge. Which in itself creates an apathy towards learning for pleasure.

Getting it right is sometimes exceedingly difficult, particularly if we think about our 'personal recordings' as previously discussed in this book.

However, if we make learning interesting and fun, children will be motivated to engage on the topics they need to learn. If we make it boring, they will not engage as well.

Light Bulb Activity

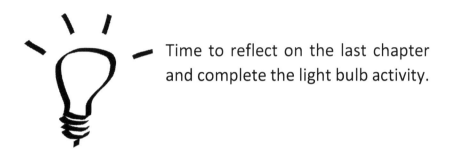 Time to reflect on the last chapter and complete the light bulb activity.

What was interesting in the last chapter?

How can this knowledge be used to your advantage?

Where and when can you implement any new ideas or plans to help with this?

Chapter Eleven

Movement to Learn, Movement to Think

"So be sure when you step, Step with care and great tact. And remember that life's A Great Balancing Act. And will you succeed? Yes! You will, indeed! (98 and ¾ percent guaranteed) Kid, you'll move mountains."

Dr Seuss

The story of Dame Gillian Lynne

Gillian's gift for dancing was discovered by a doctor. After her teachers complained that she lacked concentration at school and was under-performing as a result, her mother took her to see a doctor. She advised the doctor that

Gillian could not stop fidgeting and suffered from a lack of focus.

Apparently, after listening to Gillian's mother, the doctor told Gillian that he needed to talk to her mum in private and left her in the room alone listening to the radio. They watched Gillian dancing to music on the radio, having a wonderful time. In observing this, the doctor quickly and reassuringly advised Gillian's mum that there was absolutely nothing wrong with her daughter, however she needed to be enrolled in a dance school.

Dame Gillian Lynne had an extremely long and illustrious career as a ballerina, dancer, choreographer, actress, and theatre-television director, working on many productions which amongst many, included The Royal Opera House, The Royal Shakespeare Company and English National Opera as well performing in many West End and Broadway shows. With a huge association to the longest running shows in Broadway history; Cats, Cabaret and Phantom of the Opera, as well as Chitty Chitty Bang Bang, Gillian Lynne won numerous awards during her career including a BAFTA and a Silver Order Merit. In 1997, she was honoured with a CBE and made DBE in the 2014 New Year's Honours List for her services to Dance and Musical Theatre. This was such a huge achievement, as Gillian was the first woman in history to be honoured in this way.

In 2018, The New London Theatre was renamed the Gillian Lynne Theatre, making it the first theatre in the West End of London to be named after a non-royal woman. Sadly, this was the same year that Dame Gillian Lynne passed away at the age of 92.

Having been negatively branded by her school, Gillian Lynne was so lucky to have been sent to the doctor. Her talents were truly recognised that eventful day, with Gillian going on to inspire and influence millions of people for decades to come.

Sadly, we have become conditioned over hundreds of years to believe that some professions are better than others, based on a set of criteria that has no bearing on happiness and personal interest.

So why are some subjects not considered as important?

Too many children are branded incorrectly by the system, and then branded as disruptive or having a disorder, as they struggle to conform to the fixed agenda set by the governing bodies. There is extraordinarily little consideration for the need to exercise, sing, partake in physical activities and stretch the brain in different ways. These are also extremely important for a sound mind, as we all know. During the COVID-19 pandemic, one of the things that everybody was desperate to keep was daily exercise. Similarly, the global obsession with TikTok proves that people love performing. Point made.

It is hardly surprising that so many children suffer from low self-esteem, depression, and anxiety. They desperately need a work-life balance of academic, vocational, and physical subjects.

The whole drive of education should be to generate happy children and in turn, happy adults with a high self-esteem and self-worth.

We know that schools invest money for playground equipment, climbing frames and sports facilities; however, we seem to have missed that introducing this into the way we teach will excel learning, stimulate the mind and create happier soles.

Can you imagine an activity for measuring shapes and angles that was different to sitting in a classroom and watching the teacher present information on a white board, followed by individuals completing a mundane workbook activity?

Just imagine an interactive activity held outside to deliver the same outcome. This could be achieved in the playground in teams. They are given tasks, like draw the climbing frame equipment, or playground measurements, label and measure all the shapes and add up the whole area. This could also be followed by an activity of how would you improve or develop the areas? This activity achieves so much more than the traditional method as it combines Maths with creativity, awareness, team building, communication, and collaborative working. This is the type of thing children need to learn for later life in organisations and businesses. However, the most important part is that it stimulates the learning process by using kinaesthetic methods that in turn accelerate the learning. This is not difficult to do, however the positive impacts on learning could be a huge advantage for all.

All children are born knowing that learning is fun; however, through our education system some find out that it is no longer fun, and children that never learn this are our lucky ones.

Learning is fun, we just get taught somewhere along the line that it is not!

It is no wonder if our child happens to be less academic and more practical, we set them up to fail in the eyes of our education system. By the time they get to secondary education, the resistance to learn is already set and thereafter the pressure is on.

Research has proved that the brain is like a wiring system and is developing and growing continuously from the moment we are born. The more we use it, the better the signalling is and that the more stimulus our brain gets, the more it will develop.

We all have differing abilities and a multitude of talents, and when our child is born we watch them closely every second to see how they are developing. We read books, speak to family members, friends, and professionals to gain reassurance that the child is 'on track' to being a capable and confident being, that will be able to one day stand on their own two feet and lead a happy and successful life in whatever they choose.

It is also not rocket science that we, as parents, love our children, so in turn, we want them to achieve and do well in everything they do. We also take other people's opinions into consideration, particularly the experts in education who have studied for several years on particular subjects, enabling them to transfer their knowledge to our youngsters.

What is the main flaw in this? The governing bodies benchmark all schools and children against the same criteria, regardless of their natural talents. The curriculum and levels set to such complicated standards within governments, resulting in the teachers trying to deliver to such varying levels of capability which is virtually an impossible task.

This is when learning starts to become boring for the children, as teaching large numbers and many that may be struggling to achieve far more complex levels than really required for the age group, just becomes a battle. That is when learning stops being interesting and fun and just becomes a frustration.

As we know, there are many inspirational teachers, in fact, we can probably all reflect back on them with admiration and respect. However, working in a stringent and antiquated system is stifling for too many of our teachers and children can never become what they deserve to be.

I am sure there are so many factors as to the comments in my previous sentence, however some of the influences must be the government's curriculum in relation to how they measure the success of a school and in turn the teachers within. When we say the word SATS, most parents blood runs cold as this may give us some indicators as to what the government believe to be important factors in a child's development. But it is certainly not the be all or end all.

We should be recognising and celebrating the differences of all our children and educating them accordingly with the most important aim being that 'they believe in themselves'.

By stimulating all the senses and all Intelligences, we provide enjoyable and sustainable learning solutions that learners enjoy.

Light Bulb Activity

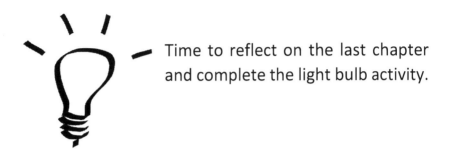

Time to reflect on the last chapter and complete the light bulb activity.

What was interesting in the last chapter?

How can this knowledge be used to your advantage?

Where and when can you implement any new ideas or plans to help with this?

Chapter Twelve

Being Branded with a Disorder

"If you have kids who are struggling with dyslexia, the greatest gift you can give them is the sense that nothing is unattainable. With dyslexia comes a very great gift, which is the way your mind can think creatively."

Orlando Bloom

As some readers of this book will already know, when your child is diagnosed as having a learning disorder or special need, it can be heart breaking, as immediately we start to imagine all of the struggles they may potentially face throughout their lives.

What we fail to see is that a learning difference, termed as a 'disorder' in our mainstream education, is an obstacle for the system and in turn the teachers, as they are automatically challenged with high numbers in their class, along with a rigid curriculum and perhaps facing failure, not only for their class but the whole school.

In turn, this creates potential anxieties in our children, as they may find the way in which they are taught challenging for the way their brain takes and receives information as previously explored.

However, research has proved that many disorders actually have great advantages in life.

There are many learning disorders that have been identified, however I have concentrated for the purpose of this book on the two most widely referenced in our schools: Dyslexia and ADHD.

Definition of Dyslexia is:

A general term for disorders that involve difficulty in learning to read or interpret words, letters, and other symbols, but that do not affect general intelligence.

There are a few key points in the above statement, however the most important for a parent to grasp is that dyslexia does not mean a child is not intelligent.

In fact, it is well documented that people diagnosed with dyslexia have many great talents in many areas. Some may include having strong three-dimensional abilities and a fantastic imagination. This can often be seen in their ability to build creative models using tools like Lego. Others may be talented at creating exciting stories, again using their imagination, and making up jokes that make people laugh and have fun. It could be that they are able to quickly show empathy and the ability to understand others' emotions (Emotionally Intelligent – high EQ), which in turn enables them to build strong relationships. It is also well documented that children with dyslexia are often innovative in science, as they have the ability to think outside the box, being creative in problem solving. This is because they use their ability to imagine alternatives and then influence and lead people with their inspirational thinking.

The list goes on and if you have a child who has been diagnosed as dyslexic, you will probably recognise some of the traits they have that make them stand out from the crowd.

"I like to think I have a superpower called dyslexia. I am creative, intuitive, and empathetic. I am great with problem solving, and I can think outside the box."

Lorin Morgan-Richards

There is a fantastic book that explains dyslexia and all of the benefits that I would highly recommend for parents called *'The Dyslexic Advantage'* by Dr Brock L. Eide and Dr Fernette F. Eide.

This book refers to many examples of the dyslexic brain having huge advantages. They point out that amongst many advantages, that there are endless accounts of people with dyslexia who go on to being extraordinarily successful entrepreneurs and build very lucrative businesses. However, in our education system, they are considered to have 'special needs' or 'Special Educational Need' (SEN).

As previously mentioned, this label can have damaging effects for too many children's self-esteem and self-belief, for so many differing reasons. It tells them they are different and not always different for positive reasons. We really need to change that perception in our schools if we want to generate confident adults from our education system who believe that they can achieve and add value to all parts of society and the careers they choose; because they can!

In fact, many people with a dyslexic brain can easily learn how to overcome their linguistic challenges, if they are taught in the right way and this can be easily introduced into the lessons within a classroom discretely. Moreover, there is a strong argument to say we must re-design all our learning in mainstream schools to enable everybody to learn, whatever their brain preferences may be.

Teachers and schools can be creative in how they do this and some of the fixes are minor tweaks, by changing the delivery methods of the subject matter.

Now I would like to explore ADHD.

ADHD is not a disability.
It's a different ability

Definition of ADHD

Attention Deficit Hyperactivity Disorder is a behavioural disorder that includes symptoms such as inattentiveness, hyperactivity, and impulsiveness.

The symptoms are:

Impulsivity, hyperactivity, and inattention

Children can be diagnosed as having these conditions on an individual level, for example they may just have 'impulsivity' or they may have mixed subtypes such as 'impulsivity' and 'hyperactivity'.

Definitions of these 'conditions' are:

1. Impulsivity
Acting or done without forethought or acting as an impulse.

2. Hyperactivity
The condition of being abnormally or extremely active or constantly active and sometimes with disruptive behaviour, occurring primarily in children.

3. Inattention
Lack of attention; distraction or failure to attend to one's responsibilities; negligence.

Experts on ADHD would say that the disorder manifests in various ways, depending upon the subtype. The most common is children with the inattention subtype resulting in them being too easily distracted and have difficulty controlling their attention, but they do not display hyperactive or compulsive behaviour. With the hyperactive-compulsive subtype the child displays unacceptable, high levels of physical activity and has difficulty controlling their behaviour in a way that is appropriate for their age!

Another opinion may be that these are normal behaviours for children and they just require more stimulation!

Many children just have a need for more physical activity to stimulate their brain and learn in a physical way, as do many adults in my experiences.

Importantly, to diagnose symptoms, these 'problems' must be displayed in at least two separate places, for example at home and at school, over at least a six-month period, and between the ages of 6 and 12 years.

This means this disorder is intrinsically linked to the environment. The questions assessed are; *'how appropriate is the child's behaviour in any given situation'*, and *'what is the impact of that behaviour to the situation?'* There is no physiological diagnosis of ADHD.

Interestingly, in the United Kingdom, there are approximately three times as many boys than girls diagnosed with ADHD and more research does need to be undertaken into this. Although some would say this may be because girls are less susceptible, however as the same diagnostic criteria is used, some people think this is not an accurate or good benchmark.

We do know that there are continuous debates on whether the condition is more linked to what people believe to be acceptable levels of behaviour, and have these levels changed as to what is assumed to be 'not acceptable' both from parents and teachers.

Another interesting fact is that ADHD tends to run in families and although there is no identified genetic fault, research has shown that parents and siblings of a child with ADHD are more likely to have had the condition themselves.

The facts remain that ADHD is labelled a disorder.

Some people may challenge the condition altogether and question the fact that it is absolutely normal for anybody, including children, to get distracted and find it hard to concentrate, particularly if they have something better to think about, or even more likely, when they are bored. Some would say they are badly behaved; however, for many of these children overcoming their boredom is easily resolved if we can made school fun, enjoyable with more activities in learning. Everybody would benefit.

So why is this all so important?

As adults, if we do not see the relevance of something to our work or life, we generally show it little interest, if any at all. For children, unfortunately classroom teaching can be generally boring, let alone young children who have gone from being at home or kindergarten where they have been exploring physically and mentally by touching, tasting and smelling (kinaesthetically), to now being in a room with lots of other children and having to watch and listen for long periods of time with very little or no physical interaction.

In mainstream schools with high class numbers, different learning styles, diverse cultures, and inherent behaviours, it is necessary to exercise a form of 'crowd control'. So, if certain individuals are struggling with their own behaviour, then suppressing their needs can be an easier route than creating environments with reasonable and relevant levels of learning in the curriculum to ensure the child's brain is stimulated enough to learn.

We also know that it is only compulsory for schools to have two hours of physical education a week, which for many children is just not enough activity.

Some schools just do not understand the need for, nor subscribe to the benefits of, physical learning. An example of this is when my eldest daughter joined high school into year 7, the measures were so strict, that even holding a pen whilst the teacher was talking, resulted in pupils receiving a caution. This is exactly the opposite remedy for somebody who learns physically. To remove any physical interaction, including the right to hold a pen, for so many learners can be stifling for the brain, so it just stops working.

If you reflect to when children held blankies as a comforter, it is a tool they used to reassure them everything is okay. Consider that many children find the transition from primary to high school a challenge for many reasons, then removing the ability to simply hold an object; an 'anchor' to provide a little comfort or reassurance is surely, and in fact, pointless. I guess the objective of such a restriction is to ensure classes are totally focused on their teacher, free of any distraction. However, in reality, by forbidding students from something, in the grand scale of things, as insignificant as holding a pen, the pupil is not getting the basic needs and may result in some behavioural, perhaps unruly reaction.

With all 'conditions' and 'disorders' that have been created, we have got into a trap of thinking that when a child's brain does not operate in the way in which the schools needs it to, then the child may have a disorder which is stopping them from learning.

With this belief, we have become 'conditioned' to consider that many children have disorders to learning that may require medication. Whereas in many cases, if the child was given the opportunity to learn the subject in a more active or creative way, they may not show the same signs, nor lack of concentration. One thing is for sure, there is, without a doubt, a need for much more research into physical learning methods and tools. After all, these are our children and our future.

In turn, if we then consider that many schools have reduced daily exercise activities such as physical education, games, music, crafts, art, drama and dance to enable more Maths, English and Science to meet the standards set by governing bodies, along with endless levels of homework, when do our children have a chance to exercise, build relationships with the outside world enabling them to gain all the social skills required to be a well-balanced adult? If we built in more physical learning and outside activities, we provide an opportunity for young people to exert energy and get some fresh air.

A note of interest is that...

'The NHS have explained that there is a strong connection between green space and good mental and physical health. Whether it's a local woodland area, park or by simply getting fresh air close to where patients live, doctors are encouraging people to make the most of the outdoor space around them.'

There is an initiative by doctors to prescribe more 'green space' and 'nature' to patients struggling with mental health issues. We all know that the tonic of fresh air helps our wellbeing, so why are we not doing more of this in schools?

Parents recognise this and so too do many schools, investing in outside play equipment. So, why cannot more be done to create inside activities as-well.

Society has accepted the labels that enable the education system to put backsides on seats, rather than exploring how teaching methodologies can be changed to adapt to teaching everybody, whichever way they learn.

It follows that by considering Howard Gardner's Multiple Intelligences and Kolb's / Honey and Mumford's Learning Styles, we could create better measures to unleashing the attitudes, skills and behaviours of all our children, ensuring they all are nurtured to become the best they possibly can be with their raw talent.

Of course, this would mean a complete overhaul of our education system, but then, aren't our children worth that?

Instead we have created medication to suppress conditions and help the neurons in our brain work differently by stimulating more 'neurotransmitters' between them or slow down the transmitters. The basic facts are that there are two main types of treatment used: stimulants and non-stimulants which both target a different neurotransmitter. And it is also important to realise that not all people respond equally, so frequently children are switched between the different types of medication in an attempt to get the right remedy.

It is also important to realise that by medicating our children, they may suffer from the side effects of these types of drugs, with some of the more common side effects being decreased appetite and trouble sleeping. And when the medication wears off, some children will suffer anxiety or restlessness, known as the rebound effect. Some of the less common side effects are motor tics which are defined as sudden, repetitive, nonrhythmic motor movements or vocalisation involving discrete muscle groups. They may not be noticed by other people, however in this instance, the child will suffer abdominal tensing, such as toe crunching, eye blinking and throat clearing.

It remains the case that many educators believe children that struggle to concentrate, who fidget and/or have disruptive behaviours can be supressed with medication. And that this control of their behaviour is more important than the side effects such medication has on the child, not to mention the psychological issues they might develop from being branded as having a 'problem' which makes them different!

In turn this can lead to anxiety, low self-esteem, depression, and an overall feeling that they 'don't' belong and they 'don't really fit in'. They are different and, in their minds, and unfortunately others, they are not the norm.

Although many parents are made to feel they have no alternative and yes, the child may show significant improvements in the way they concentrate, we have to ask is this really the best way forward? Or should we be exploring more holistic measures to ensure our children enjoy learning and thus engage to help the learning process?

The diagnoses figures of children with ADHD are growing globally, with many being diagnosed incredibly early on at primary school age. Intriguingly, figures also show that ADHD decreases in secondary school.

This is such an interesting subject and we do have to explore what may be behind this and what else could be done, rather than find parents in the desperate situation where they are asked to give their child drugs in order to help them concentrate and learn.

It is widely recognised that we all need exercise, activities and excitement in our lives to stay healthy, both physically and mentally, yet as the bar is set so high for schools they have no time for our young children to have fun, exercise, play and get rid of all that excitable energy.

As we know, the brain is developing rapidly during our younger years, however there are so many ways we can learn other than just sitting at a desk and listening to somebody telling us information.

We should explore other options as to what can be done differently for all subjects to ensure we engage all learners. Even if the governing bodies think they are providing a high level of education, along with some of the fortunate children and parents who thrive in the environment. There is also enough evidence that this is not the case for too many children. Without a doubt, many teachers know this too and struggle with this daily; however, they are made to meet the standards set out by the higher powers and therefore, have no option to become part of the system they find themselves in.

I would challenge that most disruptive behaviour comes from a frustrated learner. It is very natural to need various ways to be taught on any subject to get the most out of any learning intervention.

When I train adults how to present and speak publicly, I look for their natural talent; how they like to think and communicate. If they like to move to think, I encourage them to do so. This means we see the 'real' person, the 'natural' behaviours and in turn, makes their presentation interesting and engaging, rather than a robotic performance that lacks emotion and passion.

Other people will stand very still and perfectly replay from memory the content of their subject matter and perform perfectly whilst being very engaging. This is absolutely bringing out their raw talent.

We have been conditioned to believe that all children should be able to sit completely still and in silence while they are able to think and contribute to a lesson. This is just not true. This type of schooling stems from the 1800s and the Industrial Revolution, not for the 2020s.

So, the point is that many children have so many amazing talents and our role as educators is to unleash their full potential, to prepare them for adult lives and the careers paths they wish to follow. If we introduced better methods and criteria to suit everybody, or at least strive for that, we will create a far better life for many young people.

Instead, we have created a world of conformists to suit our education system, and possibly destroyed the ability for some individuals to reach their full potential in so many other subjects that fulfil them and that they may be brilliant at.

We can destroy very quickly a child's self-belief and esteem to becoming the best they can be by using stringent methods to 'manage the audience', rather than unleash all the individual's talents.

I see so many coming into my training, initially fearful and anxious that my sessions will be like their recollection of school. They are pleasantly surprised when they realise that my role is to unleash their raw talents and not to continuously measure what they cannot do, suppress their thought processes or to highlight their downsides. No, my role is to concentrate on their strengths!

Sadly, parents are often left feeling completely helpless at the hands of education system and understandably find themselves agreeing to many alternative fixes, rather than looking at the methodologies and how they could be upgraded or re-energised to create a more engaging learning experience.

The truth is that when people with dyslexia or ADHD are able to find something that they're passionate about, they will dedicate themselves as hard as anyone - often at times crushing the competition.

And judging by what some people have accomplished, I think it's safe to say that it should be considered more of an advantage than a weakness.

The following list contains people who have diagnosis of ADHD, ASD, Dyslexia or another related condition. The earliest references to an ADHD-like disorder date back to the late-18th century. Most of those still alive have specifically been diagnosed with the condition, the remainder and those who died prior to this date have been professionally diagnosed using the diagnosis rules being applied to their biographies.

TV Celebrities, Comedians, Actors & Directors

Alfred Hitchcock	Jay Leno	Ryan Gosling
Ann Bancroft	Jim Carrey	Steve McQueen
Billy Connolly	Jim Henson	Steven Spielberg
Danny Glover	Keanu Reeves	Sylvester Stallone
Dustin Hoffman	Keira Knightley	Tom Cruise
Emma Watson	Kirk Douglas	Whoopi Goldberg
George Burns	Lindsay Wagner	Will Smith
Henry Winkler	Michael Palin	Woody Allen
Holly Willoughby	Orlando Bloom	Woody Harrelson
James Stewart	Robin Williams	
Jamie Oliver	Russell Brand	

Arts

Ansel Adams	Pablo Picasso	Vincent Van Gogh
August Rodin	Salvador Dali	

Athletes & Sports

Alberto Tomba	Greg Louganis	Michael Phelps
Babe Ruth	Jackie Stewart	Muhammed Ali
Bruce Jenner	Jason Kidd	Nolan Ryan
Carl Lewis	Luke Kohl	Pete Rose
Fernando Verdasco	Magic Johnson	Terry Bradshaw
Hank Kuehne	Michael Jordan	Tim Herron

Business & Visionaries

Andrew Carnegie	John D Rockefeller	Tommy Hilfiger
Anita Roddick	Malcolm Forbes	Walt Disney
Bill Gates	Richard Branson	William Wrigley Jr
F W Woolworth	Steve Jobs	
Henry Ford	Theo Paphitis	

Literature

Agatha Christie	Jules Verne	Sir Richard Francis
Edgar Allan Poe	Jim Henson	Burton
Ernest Hemingway	Leo Tolstoy	Samuel Johnson
George Bernard Shaw	Lewis Carroll	Thomas Carlyle
Hans Christian Anderson	Mark Twain	Valerie Hardin
		William Butler Yeats

Music

Adam Levine	John Denver	Ozzy Osbourne
Bob Dylan	John Lennon	Rachmaninov
Britney Spears	Justin Timberlake	Robbie Williams
Cher	Kurt Cobain	Stevie Wonder
Elvis Presley	Ludwig van Beethoven	Wolfgang Mozart
George Frideric Handel	Michael Jackson	Will-I-Am

Politicians, World Leaders & Royalty		
Abraham Lincoln	George Bush Snr	Nelson
Anwar Sadat	George Bush Jnr	Rockefeller
Benjamin Franklin	George	Prince Charles
Dwight	Washington	Robert F Kennedy
Eisenhauer	John F Kennedy	Thomas Jefferson
Eleanor Roosevelt	Napoleon	Winston Churchill
Gamal Abdel-	Bonaparte	Woodrow Wilson
Nasser		

Scientists, Mathematicians, Innovators & Pioneers		
Alan Turing	Hans Asperger	Russell Varian
Albert Einstein	Harvey Cushing	Socrates
Alexander	Sir Isaac Newton	Thomas Edison
Graham Bell	Leonardo Da Vinci	Steven Hawking
Christopher	Louis Pasteur	Wernher von
Columbus	Michael Faraday	Braun
Galileo	Nikola Tesla	The Wright
James Clerk	Nostradamus	Brothers
Maxwell		

Light Bulb Activity

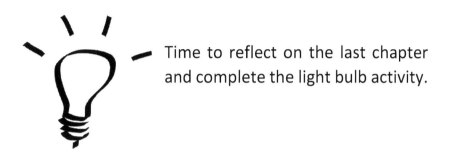 Time to reflect on the last chapter and complete the light bulb activity.

What was interesting in the last chapter?

How can this knowledge be used to your advantage?

Where and when can you implement any new ideas or plans to help with this?

Chapter Thirteen

What Employers Need?

*"Your work is going to fill a large part of your life,
and the only way to be truly satisfied is to do
what you believe is great work.
And the only way to do great work
is to love what you do."*

Steve Jobs

Over the past 30 years I have been working in businesses, and latterly the last 12 years coaching and developing many leaders within well-known organisations, enabling them to recruit and develop the right people into the right roles, creating sustainable and workable models. During this time, I have learnt, without exception, that industries and organisations require many differing skills, behaviours, and knowledge to be operationally effective.

Without a doubt, these organisations and industries require a wide range of talents and personas with many differing skills, knowledge, and behaviours. Having self-belief and a 'can-do' mentality enables them to contribute effectively to a common goal.

Many of these key competencies can be learned and trained from early years, and thus embedded over a long period. Experience and knowledge develops with time.

Frequently, I work with individuals to help them develop self-belief systems, where the learner may be lacking in confidence to complete tasks or the assertiveness to excel in their careers. And all too often my delegates share with me that they have experienced being made to feel uncomfortable, or even worse ridiculed, during some early life learning.

My role is to explore the raw talent and develop them to being the best based on that talent.

Sometimes as adults, we forget how important self-esteem and self-belief are, and without them unfortunately the person may never really shine. It also does not take a lot to make another person feel uncomfortable and in the long-term can be severely damaging to a person's confidence.

Too often we have branded children as disruptive instead of understanding them and other capabilities such as interpersonal (understanding others) and intrapersonal (understanding self) which are not widely taught in school, yet at work are vitally important in some roles that entail interacting with others.

It's time to make the change in education and create curriculums that meet the needs of adult life. If we identified the talents of individuals and capitalised on them, this would go a long way in encouraging and maintaining self-esteem and motivation. A sense of belonging.

We, in life, require a multitude of techniques, behaviours and skills, and, although it is important to have a good level of English and Maths it is also vitally important to have other skills and behaviours for life.

In fact, I work closely with a digital media agency and was interested when the Managing Director shared with me that when searching for 'creative' professionals, she often invited candidates in for interview who had spelling mistakes on the resume. In her opinion, it meant they would be more likely to be 'right brain' dominant and therefore, naturally more imaginative and creative.

Organisations consider these factors to ensure they can recruit the right people into the right roles, and ensure they keep employees by providing wellbeing support geared up to retaining their workforce. They recognise that the happiness of their employees is paramount to guarantee operational excellence.

Successful companies aspire to having a motivated and collaborative workforce, which in turn enables them to achieve their goals for a successful business model.

Although we know some schools work hard to achieve this too, there is still much work to be done to ensure the wellbeing of ALL pupils are considered in ALL schools. This must be the primary goal. Because well-balanced, valued, and confident adults create happy and harmonious neighbourhoods and organisations.

With the restrictive and stringent measures currently in place, teachers just aren't able to consider the much larger picture of balance. Instead, they are forced to adhere to the constant academic measures and make the hard decision to drop certain activities from the curriculums to meet these standards. If companies acted in the same way, they would struggle to recruit.

We, in society, have been conditioned, over many years, that the two main subjects supersede all others and if your child is not exceptional in these areas, then they are not very bright. This is not right for most businesses, yet governing bodies continue to elevate them. This alone creates too much anxiety for many children and parents, and unfortunately leads to children having limiting beliefs, anxiety and in turn, some very miserable children.

How many parents have painstakingly struggled with homework, dealt with the tantrums, and felt completely helpless when trying to complete these tasks?

Of course, everybody deserves the right to a work-life balance. They work hard at school and concentrate for up to six plus hours a day so when they come home, they naturally want to relax, ride their bikes, read a great book or comic and play with friends in the evenings and weekends. This is where they learn so many social skills and how to interact with other fellow beings in a stress-free environment. Interpersonal and Intrapersonal skills work on their Emotional Intelligences instead of sitting on a seat again to do more work, but this time at home.

The joy of reading books, comics or magazine is so important. Choosing something they enjoy reading rather than being told what to read. As we know from the research previously mentioned in this book by Professor Stephen Krashen, if children are given time to have 'Enjoyable Voluntary Reading' they gain all the literacy skills they need for life.

Although discipline to get tasks achieved and to stretch ourselves beyond our basic capabilities is important. If we expected our workforce to continuously come home and work for another few hours in their spare time, we would soon see the cracks in surface and potentially, employees would complain that they were overworked to levels where they felt stressed. So why then, is it okay to enforce this for hours on our children? Because we have been conditioned to believe this helps them achieve high academic standards and therefore it is acceptable. And as previously mentioned some learners may enjoy this, however research is proving that homework can be counter productive

According to the infographic below, created by Ozicare Insurance, the countries that offer the best education systems around the world don't always dole out piles of homework to students.

For example, Finland has short school terms and extended holidays, and the country limits the homework load to 2.8 hours total of homework per week. Despite their educational system, Finland manages to rank among the top countries in math and science innovations, and also with a smaller drop-out rate. Due to their approach on education, students feel a lesser burden imposed on them thus embracing learning.

Even better, Finland's educational system discourages cramming of concepts and trains teachers to impart lessons to students in a matter that they understand the information equally.

In Italy, whose education system ranked relatively low on the 2014 Pearson review, complete about 8.1 hours of homework per week, while students in South Korea, whose education system ranked number one in the world on the 2014 Pearson review, only spend 2.9 hours on homework weekly.

It is also well documented that by assigning more homework to children, the level of anxiety increases which leads to low motivation in schoolwork. As such, the productivity and attitude of kids towards education is lowered, which in turn leads to more drop-out rates and lesser grades.

We also have alarming rates of obesity and immorality in kids, less homework creates more parent and child time and allows children to engage in more co-curricular activities. As such, parents get a chance to instil moral character in kids, and also involve kids in sports and exercise.

And, although there are many young people who thrive in this way, too many do not, and it is like being disciplined day after day.

It is really all about balance, there should be life choices and empowerment for everybody. This in turn grows self-worth and self-esteem, something lacking in too many children.

Although in successful organisations there are often clear goals and close measures, they also must consider their reputation as an employer. They recognise that people need to want to work for them in order to get the best employees. If employers constantly criticised and embedded a fear of failure where nobody would come up with new ideas and improvements, the companies would stagnate and eventually disappear.

We have legalised this constant scrutiny of our children, with constant academic measures, ruthlessly, with no consideration to what this does internally to their inner happiness. The mindset is that 'the professionals and academics must know best' so let's not challenge it, after all we need to keep up with the developing markets.

This is just not true and there needs to be a complete review of what we teach, why we teach it and how this can be applied in the real world.

Creative writing is fantastic to stimulate the imagination. This enables a child to express themselves, and if the odd word is misspelt, how important is that really? What is the most important part here? That the child can transfer their fantastic imaginative ideas onto paper or that they can spell every word perfectly?

After all, accountants and copywriters are an extremely important part for any business, however, so are creative sales and marketing professionals, engineers, human resource specialists with exceptional communication skills and abilities to build rapport and strong relationships.

Light Bulb Activity

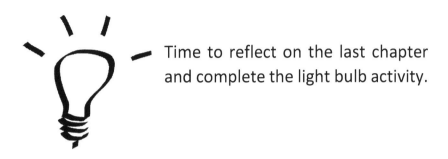 Time to reflect on the last chapter and complete the light bulb activity.

What was interesting in the last chapter?

How can this knowledge be used to your advantage?

Where and when can you implement any new ideas or plans to help with this?

Chapter Fourteen

In Summary

"Young children are wonderfully confident in their own imaginations...

Most of us lose this confidence as we grow up."

Sir Ken Robinson

As our children develop, some maintain the belief that learning is fun, however too many learn that it is not fun at all, it is just too difficult.

All children have unique talents and too often their true talent is never unleashed. They are branded as 'not being very bright' or 'having some disorder' because they are struggling with the system that has been enforced upon them, which develops mainly using the left hemisphere of the brain. If your child, although extremely talented, finds academia more challenging, they are branded as not bright or even lacking in intelligence or, even worse, they have needs outside of the normal classroom capabilities.

We have not spent enough time considering the emotional and mental impacts of how we teach and for too many the whole experience is negative. We have to remember that every person needs to feel they belong and are accepted in society.

The facts are that many successful businesses are founded by young adults who left school without achieving high academic results or qualifications, along with many that are founded by the academically gifted. Governments and society have a duty of care to remove this stigma and grow the raw talents of our children as we are potentially restricting 'brilliance' and 'greatness' and, even worse, making many children feel useless for the world in which they live. After all, everyone needs to know where they fit into the big picture; their meaning in life.

I believe we need to change the way in which we measure success to enable all children to learn, feel they add value and can blossom by strengthening their raw talent. We should recognise this.

All too often, we label people with conditions such as dyslexia or ADHD amongst many others in a distorted view to make them fit into our antiquated educational system.

These conditions exist due to the criteria that we measure, pressuring the way we teach. We use this benchmarking and place greater importance on certain subjects above others, and over many years, we have conditioned our children from a very early age that they are bright, clever, or not, based on limited information and a set of criteria. This criteria has been set without enough research into exactly what it is that we want the outputs to be, except for grades in certain subjects.

Our children follow a set curriculum and that is where often opinions of other parents, teachers, family, and friends come from as to whether our child is talented or not talented.

This is unfortunately how society condition our children and sometimes almost competitively, comparing our child's development to other children, whilst paying very little attention to the happiness and mental wellbeing of the child.

Often the hierarchies that implement the academic measures for teachers are themselves academics with little consideration of how we learn and more for what results we can measure. Metric results! There is little thought as to the impact on our children's self-esteem and something completely out of a parent's control to remedy.

All of which is completely avoidable.

Possunt Quia Posse Videntur

They can because they believe they can

Everybody knows we need academically talented people in our world; however, we do not need a world just of academics, this would be impossible anyway.

We all know that the ability to write, spell, add up and take away (rudimentary mathematics) is important, of course it is; however the level to which we measure these skills and the value we put on them far outweighs what is required in the real working world and commercial environments for so many people.

Our teaching methods of 'procedural learning method' is not conducive to so many brains as it concentrates mainly on the left side of the brain, and leaves the right brain unstimulated, hence becoming a problem for many people to decipher information into any form of context and, in turn, the ability to retain the information. This is something I will explore later in the book.

I believe we need to completely change the way in which we teach to enable all children to learn, and in turn the terms 'learning difficulties' and 'special needs' will reduce dramatically.

Too frequently we hear terms like dyslexic or ADHD in a negative way, instead of a positive way, and tapping into how the brains of people really work and what can be adapted to support them to bring out the best to the advantage of everybody. Branding does not need to be negative; everybody brings something to the table.

As our children develop, some maintain the belief that learning is fun; however too many learn that it is not fun at all – it is just too difficult – and a method used by others to measure their successes and failings as a human being. All children have unique talents and too often their true talent is not being unleashed. Too many children are then branded as 'not being very bright' or 'having some disorder' because they are struggling with the system that has been enforced upon them, which develops mainly using the left hemisphere of the brain. If your child, although extremely talented, finds academia more challenging, they are branded as not bright or even lacking in intelligence or, even worse, they have special needs.

We have all discussed the development stages of our children with friends, family, and colleagues, comparing them rightly or wrongly to reassure ourselves that they are where they should be for their age. Delighted with their first word, crawl, walk; excited by their first Lego tower or picture, the first time they played an instrument making the loudest out of tune crescendo. Children do not care if they get things wrong, they will try and try again. Developing means we all get things wrong, however, at some point, children learn that getting things wrong is negative and I believe this is our main mistake in development.

If a child attempted to walk and we told them off if they fell, the experience of walking would become negative. So, we encourage them and when they fall, we pick them up, comfort them and then encourage them to walk again. Much to our delight, when they do walk, we praise them and call everyone to tell them the great news. This is positive conditioning.

When a child is learning to spell, we sit them at a table for long periods of time and teach by telling and asking the child to listen. When they get the spelling wrong, we tell them and then we test them continuously to establish how 'bright' or how 'not bright' they are. We know this is negative conditioning. We must find a better way.

We have all experienced the highs and lows of the education system, have felt proud, happy, elated and at times helpless, out of control and desperate. We know that education is the source of power; everybody should have the right to learn how to read, write and add up, subtract, multiply and divide, and most people would share this opinion.

Between birth to the age of seven we learn more than during the rest of our lives. Babies learn to crawl, then walk and toddlers learn to run. We learn colours, tastes, smells, smiles, disappointment and happiness, trust and safety, fear, and anger. How do we take all of that information in? Through our senses! And stimulating all of our senses makes our brain enjoy learning and accelerates the whole process.

At this point, you may say that's obvious and not a surprise at all and yes, you're absolutely right! So, if this is the case, why does this trend not continue throughout our early school education? Surely, we are developing our children's raw talents; or are we?

We know that many teachers try hard to make learning fun and enjoyable. However, with the constant governing measures in place to judge schools on academia and to establish where they stand in league tables, can only have knock-on effects on how schools are managed. Although we must measure schools to ensure our education is effective, we have to challenge whether the measures are correct and right for society and all young people in the education system, and whether it prepares them in a positive way for later life.

In mainstream education we have forgotten the importance of physical crafts, such as woodwork, pottery, art, dance, drama amongst many others. Subjects that provide so much Intrinsic Motivation yet are downgraded to being less important or for the 'not-so-clever' learners. These subjects are not considered as critical, and are not measured by the government to the same levels of Maths, English and Science, so much so that they sometimes don't exist in schools, as teachers are now extremely stretched to unbelievable academic targets, and there really is no time for them.

We have created a system where everybody thinks they need to go to university and get a degree to be accepted as a bright or clever person, which in life, for many roles, is just not the case.

Our education system needs time to reflect and explore better ways of teaching and upskilling our young people to become well-adjusted and content adults who enjoy the careers they find themselves in later in life, and this can only be done by growing the raw talent they are born with.

Light Bulb Activity

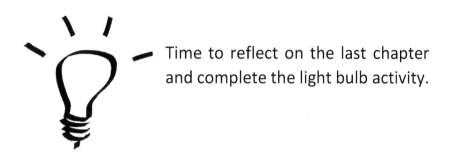

Time to reflect on the last chapter and complete the light bulb activity.

What was interesting in the last chapter?

How can this knowledge be used to your advantage?

Where and when can you implement any new ideas or plans to help with this?

Chapter Fifteen

The CRAFTS Model

*"History will judge us by the difference
we make in the everyday lives of children."*

Nelson Mandela

A good measure to ascertain why a learner may not be engaging well in the education process, is to consider where the stumbling blocks might be.

By concentrating first on Intrinsic Motivation, we are aiming in our education to use carrot before stick.

If you, or somebody you know, is being negatively branded for not being bright, disruptive or even worse, having a disorder that they will potentially be labelled with for life, then consider the following steps of the CRAFTS Model and whether something is not right in their world for learning.

Generally, there are always reasons why we see a learner struggling, and as educators it is our responsibility to get to the bottom as to why they are finding the topic challenging. Education is about offering enough blend of subjects at the right levels so that everybody gets somethings from the process.

Our role as teachers is to find an individual's raw talent and then to grow and develop it with a view to unleashing their true potential. The critical part of this is to remove any negative branding they have and help them realise where they can flourish in the world of learning. As we know, currently we are in a system where 'one size fits all' and to support this, the system is full of critics and stringent tests particularly on a narrow area of academia to constantly send a message to our children that they are really bright, not that bright, struggling or have a special need of some kind. The psychological effects of this are that we create hierarchies and prejudice in all groups. This inevitably may lead to deeper issues, as we have already explored.

The following model will help you discuss where the stumbling blocks may be festering to help you hold meaningful conversations, enabling solutions.

These common denominators, that do not change just because you have reached the age of 16 or 18, are there from birth.

The CRAFTS Model outlines these 'musts' and they should be evident and in place to motivate any learner to want to take part in the education process.

If you are concerned about somebody you know carrying a 'negative brand' in education that is having a knock-on effect to their self-esteem, self-belief and overall motivation, then try completing the CRAFTS questionnaire at the end of this chapter.

All learning should concentrate effort in the following areas:

CRAFTS:

- **C**onfidence
- **R**espect
- **A**daption
- **F**un
- **T**hread
- **S**timulation

Confidence

The learning experience should always aim to add confidence to the learner or pupil and provide them with a sense of 'belonging' in the current environment they find themself in.

The goal here is that they feel and think that they 'fit in' to the place they are learning. Always feeling safe to ask questions and having the confidence to answer when they may think they are wrong. In order to develop, they must not fear making mistakes! They need to know they can explore and share their thoughts freely, without there being any recourse.

It is difficult to measure pupils that come up with ground-breaking ideas, innovations, theories, and new inventions, so in turn this means that educators will find it hard to measure them. So, although we have subjects such as design and technology, in some cases, the educator may consider the invention as wrong or ineffective.

However, this is how many businesses and organisations flourish, so to mark things as not good or well thought out can only be somebody's subjective opinion and not necessarily correct. This is where we can grow the confidence in our schooling – the imagination.

In life, generally we get the behaviour back that we decide to display ourselves. An example of this would be a learner entering a classroom when already apprehensive, as they are unsure of what will happen to them. Possibly, they have had a previous negative experience, so to find themselves again in the learning environment, they are automatically apprehensive. The tutor's role in that instance is to provide a safe, friendly, and encouraging environment. If this is not created, for whatever reason, the learner will naturally become extremely uncomfortable and generally not take part.

There in body but not in spirit!

Even before they begin to learn they feel nervous and unsure of what is going to happen to them. A sense of belonging is critical to all learners, they feel they belong where they find themselves and they know they are safe to develop, make mistakes, say the wrong answer, and explore.

Respect

Behaviour breeds behaviour so the learning environment must be one of assertion, dignity and wellbeing as well as expecting respectful conduct, must go both ways. Learner and teacher must always interact in a respectful way, and in the events when the learner may lose their way on this matter, the teacher must always lead by example and think, *stimulus, response* and *freedom to choose* how we react.

However, this is sometimes easier said than done as teachers are only human and the moment any bad behaviour is mirrored back, it's a lose-lose situation. This is why it is important to set parameters of how everybody will behave in the learning environment, whatever the age group. If a learner has a tendency to resort to juvenile ways, then the teacher should adopt rational and reasonable adult behaviours to maintain assertiveness and dignity.

'Behaviour breeds behaviour'

The gains of insisting on a respectful and open environment creates a safety blanket for all. Enabling children to feel safe and respected, generally means the teacher will get the same behaviour back. After all, 'Behaviour breeds Behaviour'. Remember, it is good to get things wrong, that's how they learn and often shows we are trying new things.

Adaption

This area ensures that all learning has been designed to complement the needs of all the learners.

Learning styles are important here, and consideration has been given as to whether additional documents and assistance should be made available to provide help in all areas of the learning journey. Importantly, that the teacher has made plans prior to the lesson to ensure they have the right tools and information for all learning styles attending the class.

Last minute changes to material should not be suddenly positioned without clear explanation as to what has changed, and clear direction given to avoid unnecessary difficulties for certain learners.

This is where pre-lesson material can be provided to everybody prior to class. Even if only a handful of students use it, it provides some learners with prior knowledge as to what the lesson is about. For some people who like time to reflect and think, this helps them prepare their brain for the subject.

If additional information is required during the lesson, then it should be planned and given to all the learners. If they need more information, explanation, or support, build this into the lesson. Because the consequences of not preparing and including everybody highlights to the individual that they are 'different'. This conflicts with 'confidence' and the need to feel comfortable and that they 'fit in'.

By adopting the mindset that everybody is unique and that we all learn in different ways, encourages teachers to design the methods of delivery in several ways to complement all.

Fun

How many times have you attended a meeting or presentation and felt very bored? In fact, you may have even experienced the 'heavy eyes syndrome'. Learning should be stimulating and fun. Are the learners enjoying learning? What activities have been put in place to make it not only interesting, but pleasant, interactive, and also exciting?

What considerations have been given for group activities, experiments, discussions, small break-out groups with key roles within the groups, as well as individual learning and watch and hear sections?

Considerations for physical and emotional learning to take place is vital for so many learners to enjoy the experience, ensuring that all the senses are stimulated.

If the student is relaxed and engaged enough to learn, what methods have been set to ensure this is happening?

Thread

It's vitally important there is a common theme and a good 'roadmap' from start to finish of the subject being learnt. What is the aim of the learning and what outcomes will we expect to have from the class?

What is the purpose of each stage of the journey and how does it build? What is the aim of what you are hoping to achieve by the end of the lesson or subject and how does this fit into the big picture? What is the objective of why you are learning something? For example, we are learning about 'great speeches' – why is that important for the learner? Is it to learn grammar? And if so, how does that help them in their lives or is it to help them become a great speaker? What is the end result that is expected?

And finally...

Stimulation

Making sure that the learning is not boring, and it taps into all senses to ensure the brain is working across both the right and left hemispheres to stimulate the whole brain. This makes the experience interesting and engaging.

It is also important that the learners are stretched towards a goal, creating a sense of achievement.

What does the learner want to achieve from learning the subjects? How can they use this in life? What is in it for me? (WIIIFM)

So, although the CRAFTS Model is the beginning of a journey for you to establish and identify why a person you know, or even yourself, may have stumbling blocks when learning, it is important to understand why somebody may become disengaged to learning.

When assessing your own challenges, or the challenges your child is facing in education, using the CRAFTS Model may help you assess and identify ideas of how you can influence this moving forward.

Activity

Take the Questionnaire

The aim of the following questionnaire is to help you analyse where you are happy and where improvements can be made to assist in making your education valuable and enjoyable for you.

Once you have completed the sections, I would suggest these can be used as positive talking points and actions with your teachers and school.

You can answer the sections thinking about school in general, or a particular subject or teacher that you are finding challenging.

For each section you will be asked to tick a box as follows:

SA   -   Strongly Agree
A   -   Agree
D   -   Disagree
SD   -   Strongly Disagree

Please note - you can only tick one box

Section One

Confidence	SA	A	D	SD
I think the atmosphere in school / class in relation to the teachers is positive and good?				
I feel comfortable to answer a question even when I do not know the answer?				
Most of the time I feel/think that I fit into the school and can add value to the subject/s				
When asked a question I am happy to have a go at answering even if I am unsure of the correct answer?				
I have a good group of friends that I feel I can be myself with				
I think school is trying to make sure I am a better person with a strong sense of self-belief				
Total				

What observation have you taken and discussed from this section?

Respect	SA	A	D	SD
Teachers talk to me like I am a responsible person				
The school has a strong sense of looking after everybody				
There are no favourites in my school or class				
In school and class, I always feel/think that my opinion is appreciated				
I am encouraged to have my own opinions about subjects				
If I get an answer wrong, I never feel belittled or made to feel silly by the teacher/s				
Total				

What observation have you taken and discussed from this section?

Adaption	SA	A	D	SD
When learning I always understand the subject by the end of the lesson				
I am given enough time to think things through and know what they mean				
During a lesson I think the teacher/s understand how I like to learn				
I think the classes include different ways of learning the same subject to help everybody learn				
Consideration is given to all pupils in relation to how the teacher explains something				
I am given class material before a lesson to help me prepare for the class if I choose to do so				
Total				

What observation have you taken and discussed from this section?

Fun	SA	A	D	SD
I enjoy learning as it is made to be fun and exciting				
Even when I get things wrong, I feel like I have added value				
I would like more time to enjoy experimenting and having a chance to try things out in practice				
Everybody feels they can have a bit of a laugh in class, providing we listen when the teacher needs us to				
I feel comfortable to smile and have fun when I am learning in class				
If I feel like I want to fidget, I'm okay to make notes and scribble things down to help me remember				
Total				

What observation have you taken and discussed from this section?

Thread	SA	A	D	SD
I always understand why I am learning a subject as it is made clear to me				
During a lesson I know what the teacher wants me to achieve at the beginning of the class				
If I am learning about something over a few lessons, I always understand the learning journey				
Teachers take time to explain the value of what I am learning and why it is important				
I know why I learn the subjects I am doing and where I will use the information throughout my life				
The school encourage me to ask questions when I do not understand why something is being taught				
Total				

What observation have you taken and discussed from this section?

Stimulation	SA	A	D	SD
When I'm learning I always feel switched on and interested				
The teachers make a subject exciting and relevant				
If the class is getting bored, the teacher picks up on it and discusses the matter				
I think a lot of thought goes into making learning interesting				
I feel I am learning new things in lessons that I can use in my life				
There are enough activities in classes to stop me getting bored and wanting to sleep				
Total				

What observation have you taken and discussed from this section?

Section Two

Plot your answers and observations into this section

CRAFTS	SA	A	D	SD
Confidence				
Respect				
Adaption				
Fun				
Thread				
Stimulation				
Total				

Section Three

Please answer the following from your previous sections.	CRAFTS Area
What was your highest area for Strongly Agree? This indicates everything is okay in this area of schooling	
What was your highest area for Agree? This would indicate that there may be room for improvement, however, overall you are satisfied	
What was your highest area for Disagree? This would indicate there is room for improvements in this area/s and action should be undertaken	
What was your highest area for Strongly Disagree? This would indicate that there is much room for improvement and action should be undertaken to rectify this area/s	

Section Four

CRAFTS	Comments on each section
Confidence	
Respect	
Adaption	
Fun	
Thread	
Stimulation	

From your observations and answers of the above subjects, please create your plan for actions on the next page.

CRAFTS Section	Actions that I have from this area to help me	How and when can these actions have been taken?	Who can support me?
Confidence			
Respect			
Adaption			
Fun			
Thread			
Stimulation			

Light Bulb Activity

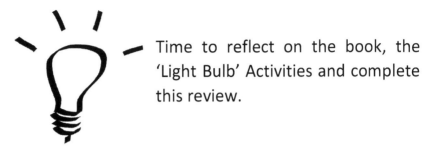

Time to reflect on the book, the 'Light Bulb' Activities and complete this review.

What are the main points of interest from this book for you personally?

How can these be used to your advantage?

Where and when can you implement any new ideas or plans to help with this?

"There is freedom waiting for you,
On the breezes of the sky,
And you ask "What if I fall?"
Oh, but my darling,
What if you fly?"

Erin Hanson

Good luck on your journey

Stay Proud

Stay Unbranded!

Printed in Great Britain
by Amazon